THE FORMATION OF THE CONSTITUTION

THE FORMATION OF THE CONSTITUTION

Edited by **ROBERT F. JONES**
Fordham University

HOLT, RINEHART AND WINSTON
New York • Chicago • San Francisco • Atlanta
Dallas • Montreal • Toronto • London • Sydney

Cover illustration: The Constitution. (*Photo Courtesy of the Granger Collection*)

Copyright © 1971 by Holt, Rinehart and Winston, Inc.
All Rights Reserved
Library of Congress Catalog Card Number: 73–146928
SBN: 03–084168–2
Printed in the United States of America
1 2 3 4   008   9 8 7 6 5 4 3 2 1

CONTENTS

George Washington presiding at the Constitutional Convention in 1787. Oil on canvas, 1856, by Junius Brutus Stearns. (*The Granger Collection*)

INTRODUCTION

To many Americans then living, the 1780s were a decade of alternating triumphs and near-disasters: the Treaty of Paris granting independence and then the subsequent low stature of the United States in world politics; the economic dislocation of the immediate postwar period and, later, the gradual recovery after 1787; the sorry record of some of the state governments in dealing with their problems and the success of others; the ineffectiveness of the Confederation Congress and the grand achievement of an apparently stable and effective government under the Constitution of 1787. Few Americans saw how the union of the thirteen states could have survived the difficulties of the 1790s without the supporting framework of the Constitution. This favorable opinion of the Constitution and its beneficent influence on American history were reinforced by the ebullient nationalism of the early nineteenth century. Even the great failure of the American system of government, the Civil War, defining by force of arms instead of force of argument the ultimate nature of the Union, showed the high regard which most Americans had for the Constitution. Neither side would allow the other to monopolize the supporting influence of its name; both the North and the South claimed to be fighting on behalf of the "real" Constitution, the one the men of 1787 had written and not the one that later politicians of the other side had distorted out of all recognition. This veneration for the Constitution was not confined to political leaders. Rather, it became part of the commonly-accepted version of American history, as this history was first written in the nineteenth century.

George Bancroft's *History of the United States* (6 vols., 1883–85) saw the Constitution as the climax of a providential plan for the union of the thirteen former British colonies. His narrative of the Philadelphia Convention of 1787 shows the Constitution as inspired as the Bible. Bancroft was not alone in this view; other less gifted and less important writers helped to drive it into the popular mind. The shock of the Civil War certainly helped to increase the Constitution's significance and value as a symbol of union. As memories of the war grew faint and as the problems of a modern industrial society began to press upon the country, however, some began to see in the Constitution a defense of property interests against popular control, an obstacle to the government's taking up the tasks of governing an industrial instead of an agrarian society. This shift of view-point had been preceded by the suggestions of several historians that the Constitution had served to check a rising popular movement in the states during the 1780s, a movement that had focused on increasing popular control of the processes of the government and the passage of various laws favoring debtors. For example, Henry Jones Ford commented in 1898 that the Constitution established "the government of the masses by the classes."[1] Writing in 1893, Woodrow Wilson pointed to the supposedly undemocratic character of the Constitution, a document drawn up by "the initiative and primarily in the interest of the mercantile and wealthy classes."[2] John Fiske's popularized history of the 1780s, *The Critical Period* (1888), probably did more than any other book to fix in the popular mind the image of an embattled aristocracy fighting off a rebellious group of farmer-debtors who had taken control of several states. It remained however for a little-noticed monograph by Orin G. Libby of the University of Wisconsin to put forward the notion that the basic division over the Constitution's adoption was economic and sectional and to support this argument by reference to a new kind of historical source, the voting records of the states. To Libby, those favoring the Constitution were concentrated in "the areas of [commercial] intercourse and wealth."[3] The opponents of the Constitution, the Antifederalists, besides being concentrated in poor, isolated areas, also favored the use of paper money and special legislation to aid debtors.

Reform-minded writers took up the suggestions of the historians and applied them in an effort to break down the popular veneration of the Constitution. In 1907, J. Allen Smith, a political scientist, pointed to the Constitution as the major barrier to the reform of American government. He wrote in order "to call attention to the spirit of the Constitution, its inherent opposition to democracy, the obstacles which it has placed in the way of majority rule."[4] Following Smith, Algie Simons, a socialist writer, attempted to demonstrate that the Constitution had come from a secret meeting, which had originated in a conspiracy, had been ratified by an undemocratic and unfair procedure, and had served the interests of "a small body of wealthy men." Simons's argument was directed to showing "that there was nothing particularly sacred about the origin of this government which should render any attempt to change it sacrilegious."[5] Thus, from suggestions by academic historians that economic motives had figured in the formation of the Constitution and that the division over its ratification had been geographic and economic, later writers progressed to the notion that the Consti-

---

1. Henry Jones Ford, *The Rise and Growth of American Politics* (New York, 1898), p. 59.

2. Woodrow Wilson, *Division and Reunion, 1829–1889* (New York, 1893), p. 12.

3. Orin G. Libby, *The Geographic Distribution of the Vote of the Thirteen States on the Federal Constitution, 1787–8* (Madison, Wis., 1894), p. 49.

4. J. Allen Smith, *The Spirit of American Government* (New York, 1907), preface.

5. Algie Simons, *Social Forces in American History* (New York, 1911), p. 9.

tution had been erected mainly to serve the moneyed men of the 1780s and in the early twentieth century was still serving that group, effectively barring the way to any meaningful and effective reform of American society.

It is doubtful that much of this viewpoint filtered down into commonly-held ideas about the origin and nature of the Constitution. Most Americans still considered it to have been handed down from on high after having been drafted by a group of demi-gods. But in 1913, Charles A. Beard, a young Columbia University professor, published *An Economic Interpretation of the Constitution*. In his book, from which the first selection has been taken, Beard applied his conception of economic determinism (a phrase he never satisfactorily defined, but which might be described as holding that the primary drive in human activities is economic) as an interpretative tool in examining the origins of the Philadelphia Convention and the subsequent ratification controversy. He described his effort as "frankly fragmentary" because of the quantity of source material that would have to be examined for a definitive study. Beard hoped this tentative work would encourage historians "to turn away from barren 'political' history to a study of the real economic forces which condition great movements in politics."[6] What Beard claimed to have found was that the Constitution was the accomplishment of a small, nationally-oriented group of men, most of whom possessed private property in the form of money at loan or public securities or had manufacturing or commerical interests, forms of property labeled "personalty" by him. The Constitution had been drafted specifically to protect these interests from the agrarian-debtors then in control of several of the states. Ratification was secured by an undemocratic procedure in the face of the disapproval of a possible majority of either actual or potential voters. Beard felt that the methods used to put the Constitution into effect constituted a "coup d'etat." His "long and arid survey" attracted immediate and mixed notice. Conservative academicians and public figures generally condemned the work for its supposed attribution of base and ignoble motives to the members of the Philadelphia Convention. But many reviewers praised the book's courageous and clear-sighted examination of the Founding Fathers' motives and actions. Practically everyone ignored Beard's characterization of his work as fragmentary and his conclusions as tentative.

What gives Beard's book special significance in the historical interpretation of the formation of the Constitution is that, during the twenty years or so following its publication, his conclusions were quietly and almost universally adopted by writers of college textbooks who, along with almost everyone else, ignored their fragmentary, tentative character.[7] Thus while many academic historians

---

6. Charles A. Beard, *An Economic Interpretation of the Constitution* (New York, 1935). p. xix.
7. Maurice Blinkoff, "The Influence of Charles A. Beard upon American Historiography," University of Buffalo *Studies,* Monographs in History, XII (May, 1936), 31.

continued to reject *An Economic Interpretation . . .* , several generations of students of American history were taught to regard it as the definitive interpretation. Beard's book had pulled off its own historiographical coup d'etat.

Recently Beard's view of the formation of the Constitution has undergone several examinations. The author of the second selection, Robert E. Thomas, has concentrated on the ratifying convention in one state, Virginia, where the Constitution provoked a very heated controversy. Beard had explained this as a duplication of the contest between, on the one hand, personalty interests and, on the other, small farmer-debtor interests found in most of the states. In testing Beard, Thomas determined the incidence of slaveholding in the Federalist and Antifederalist counties of the state and among the delegates to the ratifying convention. He also established the proportion of those in the Federalist and Antifederalist groups who had served as officers in the War for American Independence and consequently had received large quantities of Western land from Virginia. Beard had put holders of large Western land tracts down as Federalists. Thomas also determined the number of professional people (doctors, lawyers and ministers) in the opposing camps. Each of these investigations yielded a similar result: slaveholders, former officers and professional men divided almost equally on the Constitution, showing none of the overwhelming preference for the new frame of government which Beard said they had. Thomas's research led him to label the conflict in Virginia as sectional only. This said, the student may ask himself whether any sectional conflict in a state as large and varied as Virginia could be completely lacking in economic overtones. The thinly populated, developing west, in Virginia, the Piedmont and Kentucky districts, and the thickly populated, overdeveloped east, the Tidewater area, may have drawn their leaders from the same aristocratic social class, but these leaders could easily have represented the differing economic interests of their constituents. Homogeneity in slaveholding, landholding, and social status does not guarantee a homogeneity in economic interests. Thomas's data may not be as complete a rejection of the Beard thesis for Virginia as he believes it to be.

In 1961, E. James Ferguson's *The Power of the Purse: A History of American Public Finance, 1776–1790* appeared. The next year, in a critical review, Stuart Bruchey described Ferguson's work as supporting Beard's interpretation, a view Ferguson immediately denied. While refusing to be labeled a supporter of Beard, Ferguson does see the Constitution as coming from not just a need for central authority, but also a desire to check violations of property rights, the surge of unchecked majority government, and local insurrections. The situation in which the Constitution was adopted is "most adequately explained in terms of social and economic interests." The student should note that Ferguson carries on Beard's idea of a division of American society between mercantile capitalists and farmers, large and small. Considering this, how successful is he in avoiding Bruchey's charge that his book supports Beard? The exchange between Bruchey and Ferguson is included as the third selection.

The next two selections in this section complement each other directly. Orin G. Libby's study, as mentioned above, broke ground in its application of quantitative methods in historical research, specifically the use of election records to establish sectional and economic patterns in voting. Libby found that the Constitution was rejected by those living in isolated areas whose poor communications kept them from participating in the economic life of their region. He also found advocates of paper money and other measures favorable to debtors to be against the Constitution and concentrated in those isolated areas which already opposed it for physical and economic reasons. In a review of Beard's *An Economic Interpretation . . . ,* Libby continued to insist on the correctness of his view and reproved Beard for stressing economics to the exclusion of all other factors.[8] However, the student should ask himself to what extent Libby himself falls into this overemphasis. After examining the composition and political thought of the opponents of the Constitution, Jackson Turner Main, in *The Antifederalists: Critics of the Constitution, 1781–1788,* rejects Libby's contention that paper money advocates generally opposed the Constitution. He finds too many exceptions to this for it to be a valid generalization, but he does find Libby's geographical division acceptable. Main describes the supporters of the Constitution, however, not only in terms of residence but also in terms of their participation in the commerical life of their region, however indirectly. Thus commercial farmers and planters, shippers, sailors, and many city-based workers had an interest in supporting ratification for its hoped for economic effects. Those who opposed it were farmers who, either because of poor soil or poor transportation or both, were only slightly involved in their region's commerce. In Main's view this is a social as well as an economic division and supports both a class as well as a sectional interpretation of the conflict. Main also describes the Antifederalists as favoring locally-based, majority rule.

The last selection representing an economic interpretation is from Staughton Lynd's "Capitalism, Democracy and the United States Constitution: The Case of New York," which uses New York's history as a demonstration of the way in which diverse economic interests could be served by the Constitution. The prospect of an effective central government seemed to guarantee to the aristocratic leaders of New York Federalism a defense against the rambunctious democracy of their popular opponents and improved prospects for their commercial and financial interests while, to their working-class constituency, it promised some aid against the flood of foreign merchandise which threatened to swamp American markets. The Federalist leaders had been converted to nationalism by their temporary

---

8. *The Mississippi Valley Historical Review,* I (1914), 113–117.

loss of power in the state during the War for American Independence. It took an economic depression in the mid-1780s to convince the workers of New York City that a stronger central government might help to safeguard their prosperity by more effectively regulating foreign trade. Although Lynd mainly uses data from New York to support his argument, references to similarities between New York City and other American cities lead to the inference that alliances across class lines in support of the Constitution occurred elsewhere. The inter-class alliance in New York soon collapsed under the pressure of recurring class antagonisms and the return of a more normal economic situation. The existence of Lynd's lower-class Federalist supporters might not be surprising to anyone upholding the validity of Beard's thesis. New York City's small merchants and manufacturers and their workers can be seen as promoting the interests of a form of personalty, loosely defined. The student should examine this point to see if there is not a greater degree of agreement between the two authors than first seems apparent.

Thus Beard's conclusions have been modified but not rejected by these later writers. In place of a small body of nationalist conspirators, motivated by desires to fend off the attacks of agrarian democrats and to safeguard and increase the value of their special form of property, these later writers have put forward suggestions that a larger body of men, interested in promoting not just the value of personalty but rather the value of property in general, or mercantile property broadly understood, were responsible for the drafting and ratification of the Constitution. Although Beard's small body of nationalist conspirators has been expanded beyond all recognition, they are still seen as working within a framework of economic motives.

Beard's idea that economic forces condition great political movements has never been accepted by some historians who see other forces or motives as either fundamental or more significant. Differences noticed in the career patterns of Federalists and Antifederalists lead Stanley Elkins and Eric McKitrick to attribute a nationalist bias to the former. Working from a list of leading Federalists and Antifederalists compiled by Merrill Jensen,[9] Elkins and McKitrick point out that the Federalists were markedly younger than the Antifederalists and had all served in the War for American Independence on the national level rather than the mainly state-oriented service of the Antifederalists. Thus when the Confederation Congress appeared to be fast drifting toward bankruptcy and dissolution, these men turned almost automatically to a nationalistic revision of the Articles as a remedy. The completion of the Constitution gave them a political initiative which they kept throughout the ratification contest. Their task was aided by the Constitution's fitting into the major outlines of the United States: republican and capitalistic. The struggle was not between ideologies or economies, but rather between energy and inertia. Although Elkins and McKitrick

---

9. Merrill Jensen, *The New Nation: A History of the United States During the Confederation—1781–1789* (New York, 1950), pp. 424–25.

stress the political ideal of union as the source of the Federalists' energy, it is obvious that the effects of a closer union of the thirteen states were not confined to politics. Have these authors correctly described the basic source of strength for the Federalists or have they fastened on some coincidental common features of the Federalists and Antifederalists and given them an importance they do not deserve?

One assumption which Charles Beard made, and which long went unchallenged, was that the Constitution was an undemocratic document, in large part a conservative reaction to the Declaration of Independence. The author of the next selection, Martin Diamond, sees no such conflict. To him, the Philadelphia Convention was intent on realizing the promise of the Declaration, popular government, by providing a republican government purged of the "defects" and "diseases" of popular government without compromising any of its principles. In Diamond's view, the framers of the Constitution were successful in their task, a verdict, he notes, shared by Thomas Jefferson and John Adams, two men who certainly should have known what the Declaration of Independence meant. The author establishes the popular character of the Constitution by examining several of its supposedly undemocratic features in order to show, first, that these features were designed to correct some of what the framers considered to be defects in democracy and, second, that in correcting these defects, they did not violate the spirit of popular government. To Diamond, part of the Federalists' motivation was the urge to fulfill the promise made in the Declaration of Independence, that the people's right to judge would be safeguarded, but in such a way that the possibility of their judging wrongly was lessened considerably. The student can contrast Diamond's portrayal of the Philadelphia Convention as an exercise in almost pure political theory with John P. Roche's depiction of the Founding Fathers as a group of rigorously practical politicians. Roche denies theory any role at all in the framing of the Constitution.

The foregoing writers—Elkins and McKitrick, Diamond, and Roche—have rejected Beard's monistic view of the motivation of the framers and insisted on considering political motives of primary significance. They agree that historians must direct their attention to the "forces which condition great movements in politics" but refuse to label these "real" forces only "economic" as Beard did.

One of the most persistent themes in the interpretation of American history has been to see it in terms of a great consensus, that is, that most Americans agreed on the wisdom and necessity of the most basic features of American life and institutions and that all conflicts took place within this broad area of agreement. Because of the peculiar advantages of starting settlement in a virtually unpopulated land and in conditions which prevented duplicating the English and European environments, Americans were able to build a society without any of the strong, exclusive, and privileged institutions and groups which hindered the growth of democratic and republican government in the Old World.

The next group of writers sees the Constitution as the result of the operation of this consensus in forging an adequate government for the new union of states. Robert E. Brown wrote his *Charles A. Beard and the Constitution* to criticize Beard's interpretation of the movement for the Constitution and to present an alternative interpretation. Brown finds it impossible to accept any of Beard's conclusions except the very general statement that the Constitution was formed to protect property. But instead of Beard's narrowly defined and held personalty, Brown sees the property protected by the Constitution as real property, the kind of property held by most adult Americans who were freehold farmers with the right to vote. The exact form the Constitution took had to be adapted to a predominantly middle-class, land-owning citizenry reasonably well acquainted with and jealous of their rights. The ratification procedure, that is, in popularly elected state conventions, was thought by the framers to be ratification by the people. In place of Beard's narrowly drafted and supported document, Brown substitutes a frame of government which looked after the property interests of most Americans and which was drafted in the realization that their assent would have to be obtained in a reasonably democratic fashion. It should be realized that, no matter how successful Brown has been in his criticism of Beard, the demolition of Beard does not establish the value of Brown's alternative explanation. Students should examine Brown's evidence separately and carefully before accepting his conclusions.

Benjamin Fletcher Wright, in the essay presented here, is intent on showing the broad range of agreement which the members of the Philadelphia Convention shared before they met. Compromise was necessary but mainly on political issues, such as the basis of representation for the states and the method for counting slaves in apportioning representatives and direct taxes. Those economic quarrels which required compromise were basically those which divided North and South, not creditors and debtors. Wright contends that such relatively easy drafting was possible then only in the United States and only because of the wide political consensus that already existed. There was only one American institution which this consensus could not accommodate, Negro slavery.

John P. Roche views the Philadelphia Convention as working in the same spirit of compromise and persuasion as a caucus of politicians bent upon accomplishing a task of basic reform. The delegates were intent not on realizing any ideological principles but rather on drafting an adequate government which would fit into the American consensus. Their past experience as politicians gave them a clear view of the limits of this consensus, and their success at fitting a frame of government to it was one of the Federalists' major advantages going into the ratification contests. Only Negro slavery lay outside this consensus. Ultimately it could not be resolved within the framework of the Constitution. Throughout his essay, Roche fastens on the skill of the Federalists as practitioners of the art of the possible, politics. Again, the student should contrast this interpretation with that of Martin Diamond, who views the Philadelphia Convention almost as an exercise in political theory, and should ask himself whether the framers were quite as pragmatic as Roche paints them.

The idea that Americans held a basic consensus on the nature and aims of their society does not rule out the possibility of conflict. Rather it limits the conflict which does occur to less important features of the social, political, and economic institutions of the country. And, as two of these writers explicitly point out, this consensus could not accommodate slavery, an institution which ultimately proved irreconcilable with democratic government.

Gordon Wood, the author of the last selection, sees no consensus at all in the view Americans held of their society. To him, none of the previously mentioned divisive factors can adequately explain the division over the Constitution. The division between Federalist and Antifederalist was one which cut across economics and sectionalism and ranged on the one side those who believed in aristocracy, the Federalists, and on the other, those who believed in democracy, the Antifederalists. The Federalists were defending an organic society in which all men were related to each other and in which the aristocracy, a class marked not only by property but by other attributes as well, assumed for itself the task of ruling and speaking for the people. The Antifederalists answered that society was made up of interests and classes, no one of which could claim the right to speak for the other. In place of the homogeneous society the Federalists saw, the Antifederalists envisioned a heterogeneous society in which all classes and all interests had to be represented, thus taking away the social basis on which aristocratic republicanism had rested. The Federalists succeeded in getting the Constitution ratified because their opponents were unaccustomed to the tasks of political leadership. But the willingness of so many to challenge or reject the Constitution cast doubt on the future stability of the aristocratic republican society the Federalists were trying to safeguard.

In the years since the appearance of Charles Beard's work on the formation of the Constitution, historians have followed his advice to search out the "forces which condition great movements in poltics." Although many of them have refused to accept his description of these as economic, they all owe him a debt for directing the attention of the profession away from one-dimensional political history to a more varied and probing portrayal of our national history. This multifaceted inquiry is certainly a more adequate tool for understanding what the men of 1787 were trying to do and how they managed to do what they did.

After a careful reading and consideration of the selections presented here, the reader should direct his attention to the following questions: What did the Federalists who drafted the Constitution and saw it through the ratification contests want the new frame of government to achieve? Why did the Antifederalists oppose the Constitution?

To this task the student should bring the realization that no two men studying exactly the same body of source material would bring away exactly the same conclusions from their researches. It should not be surprising then that the writers presented here disagree with each other. Working from different sources, with different goals, bringing to their tasks different interests, prejudices, and preconceptions, even living in very different times—these and other factors too numerous to mention condition a historian's work and almost guarantee that he will find it impossible to agree completely with a colleague's conclusions on a topic both have studied. This disagreement on the part of professional historians should not discourage the student. The proper goal of history is understanding, not an always-elusive definitive, final, and unchallengeable statement of the truth. To the task of increasing our understanding of our national history, a variety of viewpoints can only be an advantage, not a liability. The personal dimension which each student brings to this problem—for example, his understanding of what moves men to political action—will make almost certain that yet another "answer" to the questions posed above will be given. And the student who has learned that disagreement is the normal condition for historians will be considerably ahead of the character in Agatha Christie's *The Moving Finger* who, fresh out of school, complained that "Such a lot of things seem to me such rot. History, for instance. Why, it's quite different out of different books!" To this, her companion gave the only possible reply, "That is its real interest."

CHARLES A. BEARD (1874–1948) left Columbia
University over an issue of academic freedom shortly
after publishing *An Economic Interpretation of the
Constitution* and supported himself thereafter by
writing and dairy farming. In 1935, in a preface to a
second edition, he reaffirmed with only minor revisions
the point of view presented here. The Constitution
was the work of a small body of men united by their
common possession and concern for a special kind of
property, personalty. They drafted the Constitution
so as to put special safeguards between that kind of
property and the popular majorities then in control
of some of the states. Ratification was secured by a
procedure which effectively circumvented the wishes
of what may have been a majority of the enfranchised
voters, almost certainly a majority of the adult white
males of the country. Beard thinks the measures
employed to get the Constitution drafted and ratified
add up to a "coup d'etat."*

Charles A. Beard

An Economic Document
for an Economic End

The requirements for an economic interpretation of the formation and adoption of the Constitution may be stated
in a hypothetical proposition which,
although it cannot be verified absolutely
from ascertainable data, will at once
illustrate the problem and furnish a guide
to research and generalization.

It will be admitted without controversy
that the Constitution was the creation of
a certain number of men, and it was opposed by a certain number of men. Now,
if it were possible to have an economic
biography of all those connected with its

framing and adoption,—perhaps about
160,000 men altogether,—the materials
for scientific analysis and classification
would be available. Such an economic
biography would include a list of the
real and personal property owned by all
of these men and their families: lands
and houses, with incumbrances, money
at interest, slaves, capital invested in
shipping and manufacturing, and in
state and continental securities.

Suppose it could be shown from the
classification of the men who supported
and opposed the Constitution that there

*Reprinted with permission of The Macmillan Company from *An Economic Interpretation of the Con-
stitution* by Charles A. Beard. Copyright 1913 by The Macmillan Company, renewed 1941 by Charles A.
Beard. Pp. 16–17, 149–151, 153, 169–177, 178–179, 186–188, 237–238, 240–242, 324–325. Footnotes omitted.

was no line of property division at all; that is, that men owning substantially the same amounts of the same kinds of property were equally divided on the matter of adoption or rejection—it would then become apparent that the Constitution had no ascertainable relation to economic groups or classes, but was the product of some abstract causes remote from the chief business of life—gaining a livelihood.

Suppose, on the other hand, that substantially all of the merchants, money lenders, security holders, manufacturers, shippers, capitalists, and financiers and their professional associates are to be found on one side in support of the Constitution and that substantially all or the major portion of the opposition came from the non-slaveholding farmers and the debtors—would it not be pretty conclusively demonstrated that our fundamental law was not the product of an abstraction known as "the whole people," but of a group of economic interests which must have expected beneficial results from its adoption? Obviously all the facts here desired cannot be discovered, but the data presented in the following chapters bear out the latter hypothesis, and thus a reasonable presumption in favor of the theory is created. . . .

A survey of the economic interests of the members of the Convention presents certain conclusions:

A majority of the members were lawyers by profession.

Most of the members came from towns, on or near the coast, that is, from the regions in which personalty was largely concentrated.

Not one member represented in his immediate personal economic interests the small farming or mechanic classes.

The overwhelming majority of members, at least five-sixths, were immediately, directly, and personally interested in the outcome of their labors at Philadelphia, and were to a greater or less extent economic beneficiaries from the adoption of the Constitution.

1. Public security interests were extensively represented in the Convention. Of the fifty-five members who attended no less than forty appear on the Records of the Treasury Department for sums varying from a few dollars up to more than one hundred thousand dollars. Among the minor holders were Bassett, Blount, Brearley, Broom, Butler, Carroll, Few, Hamilton, L. Martin, Mason, Mercer, Mifflin, Read, Spaight, Wilson, and Wythe. Among the larger holders (taking the sum of about $5000 as the criterion) were Baldwin, Blair, Clymer, Dayton, Ellsworth, Fitzsimons, Gilman, Gerry, Gorham, Jenifer, Johnson, King, Langdon, Lansing, Livingston, McClurg, R. Morris, C. C. Pinckney, C. Pinckney, Randolph, Sherman, Strong, Washington, and Williamson.

It is interesting to note that, with the exception of New York, and possibly Delaware, each state had one or more prominent representatives in the Convention who held more than a negligible amount of securities, and who could therefore speak with feeling and authority on the question of providing in the new Constitution for the full discharge of the public debt:

Langdon and Gilman, of New Hampshire.
Gerry, Strong, and King, of Massachusetts.
Ellsworth, Sherman, and Johnson, of Connecticut.
Hamilton, of New York. Although he held no large amount personally, he was the special pleader for the holders of public securities and the maintenance of public faith.
Dayton, of New Jersey.
Robert Morris, Clymer, and Fitzsimons, of Pennsylvania.
Mercer and Carroll, of Maryland.
Blair, McClurg, and Randolph, of Virginia.

Williamson, of North Carolina.
The two Pinckneys, of South Carolina.
Few and Baldwin, of Georgia.

2. Personalty invested in lands for speculation was represented by at least fourteen members: Blount, Dayton, Few, Fitzsimons, Franklin, Gilman, Gerry, Gorham, Hamilton, Mason, R. Morris, Washington, Williamson, and Wilson.

3. Personalty in the form of money loaned at interest was represented by at least twenty-four members: Bassett, Broom, Butler, Carroll, Clymer, Davie, Dickinson, Ellsworth, Few, Fitzsimons, Franklin, Gilman, Ingersoll, Johnson, King, Langdon, Mason, McHenry, C. C. Pinckney, C. Pinckney, Randolph, Read, Washington, and Williamson.

4. Personalty in mercantile, manufacturing, and shipping lines was represented by at least eleven members: Broom, Clymer, Ellsworth, Fitzsimons, Gerry, King, Langdon, McHenry, Mifflin, G. Morris, and R. Morris.

5. Personalty in slaves was represented by at least fifteen members: Butler, Davie, Jenifer, A. Martin, L. Martin, Mason, Mercer, C. C. Pinckney, C. Pinckney, Randolph, Read, Rutledge, Spaight, Washington, and Wythe.

It cannot be said, therefore, that the members of the Convention were "disinterested." On the contrary, we are forced to accept the profoundly significant conclusion that they knew through their personal experiences in economic affairs the precise results which the new government that they were setting up was designed to attain. As a group of doctrinaires, like the Frankfort assembly of 1848, they would have failed miserably; but as practical men they were able to build the new government upon the only foundations which could be stable: fundamental economic interests. . . .

It is difficult for the superficial student of the Constitution, who has read only the commentaries of the legists, to conceive of that instrument as an economic document. It places no property qualifications on voters or officers; it gives no outward recognition of any economic groups in society; it mentions no special privileges to be conferred upon any class. It betrays no feeling, such as vibrates through the French constitution of 1791; its language is cold, formal, and severe.

The true inwardness of the Constitution is not revealed by an examination of its provisions as simple propositions of law; but by a long and careful study of the voluminous correspondence of the period, contemporary newspapers and pamphlets, the records of the debates in the Convention at Philadelphia and in the several state conventions, and particularly, *The Federalist*, which was widely circulated during the struggle over ratification. . . . [It] presents in a relatively brief and systematic form an economic interpretation of the Constitution by the men best fitted, through an intimate knowledge of the ideals of the framers, to expound the political science of the new government. This wonderful piece of argumentation by Hamilton, Madison, and Jay is in fact the finest study in the economic interpretation of politics which exists in any language; and whoever would understand the Constitution as an economic document need hardly go beyond it. . . .

The powers for positive action conferred upon the new government were few, but they were adequate to the purposes of the framers. They included, first, the power to lay and collect taxes; but here the rural interests were conciliated by the provision that direct taxes must be apportioned among the states according to population, counting three-fifths of the slaves. This, in the opinion of contemporaries eminently qualified to speak, was designed to prevent the populations of the manufacturing states from shifting the burdens of taxation to the sparsely settled agricultural regions. . . .

The taxing power was the basis of all other positive powers, and it afforded the revenues that were to discharge the public debt in full. Provision was made for this discharge in Article VI to the effect that "All debts contracted and engagements entered into before the adoption of this Constitution shall be valid against the United States under this Constitution as under the Confederation."

But the cautious student of public economy, remembering the difficulties which Congress encountered under the Articles of Confederation in its attempts to raise the money to meet the interest on the debt, may ask how the framers of the Constitution could expect to overcome the hostile economic forces which had hitherto blocked the payment of the requisitions. The answer is short. Under the Articles, Congress had no power to lay and collect taxes immediately; it could only make requisitions on the state legislatures. Inasmuch as most of the states relied largely on direct taxes for their revenues, the demands of Congress were keenly felt and stoutly resisted. Under the new system, however, Congress is authorized to lay taxes on its own account, but it is evident that the framers contemplated placing practically all of the national burden on the consumer. The provision requiring the apportionment of direct taxes on a basis of population obviously implied that such taxes were to be viewed as a last resort when indirect taxes failed to provide the required revenue.

With his usual acumen, Hamilton conciliates the freeholders and property owners in general by pointing out that they will not be called upon to support the national government by payments proportioned to their wealth. Experience has demonstrated that it is impracticable to raise any considerable sums by direct taxation. Even where the government is strong, as in Great Britain, resort must be had chiefly to indirect taxation. The pockets of the farmers "will reluctantly yield but scanty supplies, in the unwelcome shape of impositions on their houses and lands; and personal property is too precarious and invisible a fund to be laid hold of in any other way than by the imperceptible agency of taxes on consumption." Real and personal property are thus assured a generous immunity from such burdens as Congress had attempted to impose under the Articles; taxes under the new system will, therefore, be less troublesome than under the old.

Congress was given, in the second place, plenary power to raise and support military and naval forces, for the defence of the country against foreign and domestic foes. These forces were to be at the disposal of the President in the execution of national laws; and to guard the states against renewed attempts of "desperate debtors" like Shays, the United States guaranteed to every commonwealth a republican form of government and promised to aid in quelling internal disorder on call of the proper authorities.

The army and navy are considered by the authors of *The Federalist* as genuine economic instrumentalities. As will be pointed out below, they regarded trade and commerce as the fundamental cause of wars between nations; and the source of domestic insurrection they traced to class conflicts within society. "Nations in general," says Jay, "will make war whenever they have a prospect of getting anything by it"; and it is obvious that the United States dissevered and discordant will be the easy prey to the commercial ambitions of their neighbors and rivals.

The material gains to be made by other nations at the expense of the United States are so apparent that the former cannot restrain themselves from aggression. France and Great Britain feel the pressure of our rivalry in the fisheries; they and other European nations are our competitors in navigation and the carrying trade; our independent voyages to China interfere with the monopolies enjoyed by other countries there; Spain would like to shut the Mississippi against us on one side and Great Britain fain would close the St. Lawrence on the other. The cheapness and excellence of our productions will excite their jealousy, and the enterprise and address of our merchants will not be consistent with the wishes or policy of the sovereigns of Europe. But, adds the commentator, by way of clinching the argument, "if they see that our national government is efficient and well administered, our trade prudently regulated, our militia properly organized and disciplined, our resources and finances discreetly managed, our credit re-established, our people free, contented, and united, they will be much more disposed to cultivate our friendship than provoke our resentment."

All the powers of Europe could not prevail against us. "Under a vigorous national government the natural strength and resources of the country, directed to a common interest, would baffle all the combinations of European jealousy to restrain our growth. . . . An active commerce, an extensive navigation, and a flourishing marine would then be the offspring of moral and physical necessity.

We might defy the little arts of the little politicians to control or vary the irresistible and unchangeable course of nature." In the present state of disunion the profits of trade are snatched from us; our commerce languishes; and poverty threatens to overspread a country which might outrival the world in riches.

The army and navy are to be not only instruments of defence in protecting the United States against the commercial and territorial ambitions of other countries; but they may be used also in forcing open foreign markets. What discriminatory tariffs and navigation laws may not accomplish the sword may achieve. The authors of *The Federalist* do not contemplate that policy of mild and innocuous isolation which was later made famous by Washington's farewell address. On the contrary—they do not expect the United States to change human nature and make our commercial classes less ambitious than those of other countries to extend their spheres of trade. A strong navy will command the respect of European states. "There can be no doubt that the continuance of the Union under an efficient government would put it within our power, at a period not very distant, to create a navy which, if it could not vie with those of the great maritime powers, would at least be of respectable weight if thrown into the scale of either of two contending parties. . . . A few ships of the line sent opportunely to the reinforcement of either side, would often be sufficient to decide the fate of a campaign, on the event of which interests of the greatest magnitude were suspended. Our position is, in this respect, a most commanding one. And if to this consideration we add that of the usefulness of supplies from this country, in the prosecution of military operations in the West Indies, it will be readily perceived that a situation so favorable would enable us to bargain with great advantage for commercial privileges. A price would be set not only upon our friendship, but upon our neutrality. By a steady adherence to the Union, we may hope, ere long, to become the arbiter of Europe in America, and to be able to incline the balance of European competitions in this part of the world as our interest may dictate."

As to dangers from class wars within particular states, the authors of *The Federalist* did not deem it necessary to make extended remarks: the recent events in New England were only too vividly impressed upon the public mind. "The tempestuous situation from which Massachusetts has scarcely emerged," says Hamilton, "evinces that dangers of this kind are not merely speculative. Who can determine what might have been the issue of her late convulsions, if the malcontents had been headed by a Caesar or by a Cromwell." The strong arm of the Union must be available in such crises.

In considering the importance of defence against domestic insurrection, the authors of *The Federalist* do not overlook an appeal to the slave-holders' instinctive fear of a servile revolt. Naturally, it is Madison whose interest catches this point and drives it home, by appearing to discount it. In dealing with the dangers of insurrection, he says: "I take no notice of an unhappy species of population abounding in some of the states who, during the calm of regular government are sunk below the level of men; but who, in the tempestuous scenes of civil violence, may emerge into human character and give a superiority of strength to any party with which they may associate themselves."

In addition to the power to lay and collect taxes and raise and maintain armed forces on land and sea, the Constitution vests in Congress plenary control over foreign and interstate commerce, and thus authorizes it to institute protective and discriminatory laws in favor of American interests, and to create a wide sweep for free trade throughout the whole American empire. A single clause thus reflects the strong impulse of economic forces in the towns and young manufacturing centres. In a few simple words the mercantile and manufacturing interests wrote their *Zweck im Recht;** and they paid for their victory by large concessions to the slave-owning planters of the south.

While dealing with commerce in *The Federalist* Hamilton does not neglect the subject of interstate traffic and intercourse. He shows how free trade over a wide range will be to reciprocal advantage, will give great diversity to commercial enterprise, and will render stagnation less liable by offering more distant markets when local demands fall off. "The speculative trader," he concludes, "will at once perceive the force of these observations and will acknowledge that the aggregate balance of the commerce of the United States would bid fair to be much more favorable than that of the thirteen states without union or with partial unions."

Another great economic antagonism found its expression in the clause conferring upon Congress the power to dispose of the territories and make rules and regulations for their government and admission to the Union. In this contest, the interests of the states which held territories came prominently to the front; and the ambiguity of the language used in the Constitution on this point may be attributed to the inability of the con-

---

*Purpose into the law — Ed.

testants to reach precise conclusions. The leaders were willing to risk the proper management of the land problem after the new government was safely launched; and they were correct in their estimate of their future political prowess.

These are the great powers conferred on the new government: taxation, war, commerical control, and disposition of western lands. Through them public creditors may be paid in full, domestic peace maintained, advantages obtained in dealing with foreign nations, manufactures protected, and the development of the territories go forward with full swing. The remaining powers are minor and need not be examined here. What implied powers lay in the minds of the framers likewise need not be inquired into; they have long been the subject of juridical speculation.

None of the powers conferred by the Constitution on Congress permits a direct attack on property. The federal government is given no general authority to define property. It may tax, but indirect taxes must be uniform, and these are to fall upon consumers. Direct taxes may be laid, but resort to this form of taxation is rendered practically impossible, save on extraordinary occasions, by the provision that they must be apportioned according to population—so that numbers cannot transfer the burden to accumulated wealth. The slave trade may be destroyed, it is true, after the lapse of a few years; but slavery as a domestic institution is better safeguarded than before.

Even the destruction of the slave trade had an economic basis, although much was said at the time about the ethics of the clause. In the North where slavery, though widespread, was of little economic consequence, sympathy with the unfortunate negroes could readily prevail. Maryland and Virginia, already overstocked with slaves beyond the limits of land and capital, had prohibited the foreign trade in negroes, because the slave-holders, who predominated in the legislatures, were not willing to see the value of their chattels reduced to a vanishing point by excessive importations. South Carolina and Georgia, where the death rate in the rice swamps and the opening of adjoining territories made a strong demand for the increase of slave property, on the other hand, demanded an open door for slave-dealers. . . .

Equally important to personalty as the positive powers conferred upon Congress to tax, support armies, and regulate commerce were the restrictions imposed on the states. Indeed, we have the high authority of Madison for the statement that of the forces which created the Constitution, those property interests seeking protection against omnipotent legislatures were the most active.

In a letter to Jefferson, written in October, 1787, Madison elaborates the principle of federal judicial control over state legislation, and explains the importance of this new institution in connection with the restrictions laid down in the Constitution on laws affecting private rights. "The mutability of the laws of the States," he says, "is found to be a serious evil. The injustice of them has been so frequent and so flagrant as to alarm the most steadfast friends of Republicanism. I am persuaded I do not err in saying that the evils issuing from these sources contributed more to that uneasiness which produced the Convention, and prepared the public mind for a general reform, than those which accrued to our national character and interest from the inadequacy of the Confederation to its immediate objects. A reform, therefore, which does not make provision for private rights must be materially defective."

Two small clauses embody the chief demands of personalty against agrarianism: the emission of paper money is prohibited and the states are forbidden to impair the obligation of contract. The first of these means a return to a specie basis—when coupled with the requirement that the gold and silver coin of the United States shall be the legal tender. The Shays and their paper money legions, who assaulted the vested rights of personalty by the process of legislative depreciation, are now subdued forever, and money lenders and security holders may be sure of their operations. Contracts are to be safe, and whoever engages in a financial operation, public or private, may know that state legislatures cannot destroy overnight the rules by which the game is played.

A principle of deep significance is written in these two brief sentences. The economic history of the states between the Revolution and the adoption of the Constitution is compressed in them. They appealed to every money lender, to every holder of public paper, to every man who had any personalty at stake. The intensity of the economic interests reflected in these two prohibitions can only be felt by one who has spent months in the study of American agrarianism after the Revolution. In them personalty won a significant battle in the conflict of 1787–1788. . . .

Turning from the question as to the extent of the economic motive in the personal element, Hamilton makes an inquiry into the more probable sources of wars among the states in case a firmer union, endowed with adequate powers, is not established. These he enumerates:

1. "Territorial disputes have at all times been found one of the most fertile sources of hostility among nations." The several states have an interest in the Western Territories, and "to reason from the past to the future, we shall have good ground to apprehend that the sword would sometimes be appealed to as the arbiter of their differences."

2. "The competitions of commerce would be another fruitful source of contention." Each state will pursue a policy conducive to its own advantage, and "the spirit of enterprize, which characterizes the commercial part of America, has left no occasion of displaying itself unimproved. It is not at all probable that this unbridled spirit would pay much respect to those regulations of trade by which particular states might endeavor to secure exclusive benefits to their own citizens." The economic motive will thus probably override all considerations of interstate comity and all considerations of international law. But that is not all; says Hamilton, in italics, *We should be ready to denominate injuries those things which were in reality the justifiable acts of independent sovereignties consulting a distinct interest.* " Commerce will have little respect for the right of other peoples to protect their interests, and it will stigmatize as an "injury" anything which blocks its enterprise.

3. "The public debt of the Union would be a further cause of collision between the separate states or confederacies." Some states would oppose paying the debt. Why? Because they are "less impressed with the importance of national credit, or because their citizens have little, if any, immediate interest in the question." But other states, "a numerous body of whose citizens are creditors to the public beyond the proportion of the state in the total amount of the national debt, would be strenuous for some equitable and ef-

fective provision." In other words, citizens who had nothing at stake would be indifferent, and those who had something to lose would clamor. Foreign powers also might intervene, and the "double contingency of external invasion and internal contention" would be hazarded.

4. "Laws in violation of private contracts, as they amount to aggressions on the rights of those states whose citizens are injured by them, may be considered as another probable source of hostility." Had there not been plenty of evidence to show that state legislatures, if unrestrained by some higher authority, would attack private rights in property? And had there not been a spirit of retaliation also? "We reasonably infer that in similar cases, under other circumstances, a war, not of *parchment*, but of the sword, would chastise such atrocious breaches of moral obligation and social justice."

These, then, are the four leading sources of probable conflict among the states if not united into a firm union: territory, commerce, the national debt, and violations of contractual rights in property—all as severely economic as could well be imagined.

To carry the theory of the economic interpretation of the Constitution out into its ultimate details would require a monumental commentary, such as lies completely beyond the scope of this volume. But enough has been said to show that the concept of the Constitution as a piece of abstract legislation reflecting no group interests and recognizing no economic antagonisms is entirely false. It was an economic document drawn with superb skill by men whose property interests were immediately at stake; and as such it appealed directly and unerringly to identical interests in the country at large. . . .

A survey of the [ratification contests in the states] yields several important generalizations:

Two states, Rhode Island and North Carolina, refused to ratify the Constitution until after the establishment of the new government which set in train powerful economic forces against them in their isolation.

In three states, New Hampshire, New York, and Massachusetts, the popular vote as measured by the election of delegates to the conventions was adverse to the Constitution; and ratification was secured by the conversion of opponents and often the repudiation of their tacit (and in some cases express) instructions.

In Virginia the popular vote was doubtful.

In the four states which ratified the Constitution with facility, Connecticut, New Jersey, Georgia, and Delaware, only four or five weeks were allowed to elapse before the legislatures acted, and four or five weeks more before the elections to the conventions were called; and about an equal period between the elections and the meeting of the conventions. This facility of action may have been due to the general sentiment in favor of the Constitution; or the rapidity of action may account for the slight development of the opposition.

In two commonwealths, Maryland and South Carolina, deliberation and delays in the election and the assembling of the conventions resulted in an undoubted majority in favor of the new instrument; but for the latter state the popular vote has never been figured out.

In one of the states, Pennsylvania, the proceedings connected with the ratification of the Constitution were conducted with unseemly haste. . . .

In the adoption of the Constitution, says James Wilson, we have the gratifying spectacle of "a whole people exercising its first and greatest power—performing an act of sovereignty original and unlimited." Without questioning the statement that for juristic purposes the Constitution may be viewed as an expression of the will of the whole people, a historical view of the matter requires an analysis of "the people" into its constituent elements. In other words, how many of "the people" favored the adoption of the Constitution, and how many opposed it?

At the very outset, it is necessary to recall that the question whether a constitutional Convention should be held was not submitted to popular vote, and that it was not specially passed upon by the electors in choosing the members of the legislatures which selected the delegates.

In the second place, the Constitution was not submitted to popular ratification. The referendum was not unknown at that time, but it was not a fixed principle of American politics. At all events, such a procedure does not seem to have crossed the minds of the members of the Convention, and long afterward, Marshall stated that ratification by state conventions was the only mode conceivable. In view of the fact that there was no direct popular vote taken on the Constitution, it is therefore impossible to ascertain the exact number of "the people" who favored its adoption.

The voters, who took part in the selection of delegates to the ratifying conventions in the states, may be considered as having been divided into four elements: those who were consciously in favor of the Constitution, those who were just as consciously against it, those who were willing to leave the matter to the discretion of their elected representatives, and those who voted blindly.

The proportions which these four groups bear to one another cannot be

determined, but certain facts may be brought out which will throw light on the great question: How many of the people favored the adoption of the Constitution?

The first fact to be noted in this examination is that a considerable proportion of the adult white male population was debarred from participating in the elections of delegates to the ratifying state conventions by the prevailing property qualifications on the suffrage. The determination of these suffrage qualifications was left to the state legislatures; and in general they adopted the property restrictions already imposed on voters for members of the lower branch of the state legislatures.

In New Hampshire the duly qualified voters for members of the lower house were authorized to vote for members of the convention, and those Tories and sympathizers with Great Britain who were excluded by law were also admitted for this special election. In Massachusetts the voters were those "qualified by law to vote in the election of representatives." In Connecticut, those "qualified by law to vote in town meetings" were enfranchised. In New Jersey, those who were "entitled to vote for representatives in general assembly;" and in Delaware, those "qualified by law to vote for Representatives to the General Assembly" were empowered to vote for delegates to their respective conventions. In Pennsylvania, voters for members of the assembly selected the delegates to the convention. In Maryland, voters for members of the lower house; in Virginia, those possessing the "qualifications now established by law;" in North Carolina, those entitled to vote for members of the House of Commons; in South Carolina, those voting for members of the lower house; and in Georgia, those voting for members of the legislature (one branch) were admitted to participation in the election of delegates to their respective state conventions.

In New York alone was the straight principle of manhood suffrage adopted in the election of delegates to the ratifying convention. Libby seems inclined to hold that this exception was made by the landed aristocracy in the state legislature because it was opposed to the Constitution and wished to use its semi-servile tenants in the elections; but this problem has not yet been worked out, and any final conclusion as to the "politics" of this move is at present mere guesswork.

It is impossible to say just what proportion of the adult males twenty-one years of age was disfranchised by these qualifications. When it is remembered that only about 3 per cent of the population dwelt in towns of over 8000 inhabitants in 1790, and that freeholds were widely distributed, especially in New England, it will become apparent that nothing like the same proportion was disfranchised as would be to-day under similar qualifications. Dr. [J. Franklin] Jameson estimates that probably one-fifth of the adult males were shut out in Massachusetts, and it would probably be safe to say that nowhere were more than one-third of the adult males disfranchised by the property qualifications.

Far more were disfranchised through apathy and lack of understanding of the significance of politics. It is a noteworthy fact that only a small proportion of the population entitled to vote took the trouble to go to the polls until the hot political contests of the Jeffersonian era. Where voting was *viva voce* at the town hall or the county seat, the journey to the polls and the delays at elections were very troublesome. At an election in Connecticut in 1775, only 3477 voters took part, out of a population of nearly 200,000, of whom 40,797 were males over twenty years of age. How many were disfranchised by the property qualifications and how many stayed away through indifference cannot be shown.

Dr. [J. Franklin] Jameson, by most ingenious calculations, reaches the conclusion that in Massachusetts about 55,000 men in round numbers or about 16 or 17 per cent of the population were entitled to vote under the law. Assuming that 16 per cent were entitled to vote, he inquires into the number who actually exercised the franchise in the years from 1780 to 1790 in elections for governor; and his inquiry yields some remarkable results. To give his conclusions in his own words: "Something like three per cent [of the population, or about one-fifth or one-sixth of those entitled to vote] took part in the first election in the autumn of 1780. During the next six years the figures remain at about two per cent only. In 1784, only 7631 votes were cast in the whole state; in the spring of 1786 only a little over eight thousand. Then came Shays' Rebellion and the political excitement of that winter brings up the votes in the spring election of '87 to a figure nearly three times as high as in '86, and amounting to something between five and six per cent of the population. The political discussions of the next two winters respecting the new federal government keep the figure up to five per cent. Then it drops to something between three and four and there it remains until 1794." . . .

In a few instances . . . the number of voters participating in the election of delegates to the state conventions has come down to us. In Boston, for example, where the fight was rather warm, and some 2700 men were entitled to vote, only 760 electors turned out to pass upon the momentous issue of the national Constitution—about half as many as voted in the next gubernatorial election.

The treatises on the Constitution do not give any figures on the popular vote for delegates to the state convention in New York, but the following partial list taken from contemporary papers shows that in some of the counties the vote ran to almost 10 per cent of the population, while in others the percentage of the electorate participating (even under the universal manhood suffrage provision) was about that in Massachusetts, namely, 5 per cent. It will be noted also that the distribution of representation in the convention was grossly unequal and decidedly unfavorable to the Anti-Federalists. The classification into Federalist

and Anti-Federalist is based upon the election returns as reported in the contemporary press, not on the vote in the state-ratifying convention.

Several conclusions are obvious from this table. Measured by the popular vote, New York was overwhelmingly against the ratification of the Constitution. With the apportionment of representation against them, the Anti-Federalists elected nearly twice as many delegates as the Federalists. The popular vote in favor of ratification was largely confined to the urban centres of New York City and Albany City, thus correcting assumptions based on the convention vote alone.

But with this decided popular vote against them the Federalists were able

FEDERALIST

	POPULATION 1790	HIGHEST FEDERALIST VOTE	HIGHEST ANTI-FEDERALIST VOTE	DELEGATES IN CONVENTION	RATIO OF DELEGATES TO POPULATION
New York County ..	33,131	2735	134	9	3,681
Westchester	23,941	694	399	6	3,990
Queens	16,014			4	4,003
Kings	4,495			2	2,247
Richmond	3,835			2	1,917
				23	

ANTI-FEDERALIST

	POPULATION 1790	HIGHEST FEDERALIST VOTE	HIGHEST ANTI-FEDERALIST VOTE	DELEGATES IN CONVENTION	RATIO OF DELEGATES TO POPULATION
Albany	75,921	2627	4681	7	10,845
Ulster	29,397	68	1372	6	4,899
Dutchess	45,266	892	1765	7	6,466
Orange	18,478		340	4	4,619
Columbia.	27,732	1498	1863	3	9,244
Montgomery . .	28,839	811	1209	6	4,806
Suffolk.	16,440			5	3,288
Washington . . .	15,647			4	3,911
				41	

to carry through their program by a narrow margin of thirty to twenty-seven. Why did so many Anti-Federalists whose popular mandate was clear and unmistakable, for there was a definite fight at the polls on the issue, go over to their enemies? Three Anti-Federalist members, who did go over and carry the day for the Federalists, John DeWitt, John Smith, and Melancton Smith, later appeared as holders of public securities; but this does not explain the event.

In Pennsylvania, the vote on the election of delegates to ratify the Constitution was apparently very slight. The dissenting minority in their famous manifesto declared: "The election for members of the convention was held at so early a period and the want of information was so great that some of us did not know of it until after it was over. . . . We apprehend that no change can take place that will affect the internal government or constitution of this commonwealth unless a majority of the people should evidence a wish for such a change; but on examining the number of votes given for members of the present State convention, we find that of upwards of seventy thousand freemen who are entitled to vote in Pennsylvania, the whole convention has been elected by about thirteen thousand voters, and though two-thirds of the members of the convention have thought proper to ratify the proposed Constitution, yet those two-thirds were elected by the votes of only six thousand and eight hundred freemen." Though the partisan source of these figures might lead one to question their accuracy, nevertheless it is hardly probable that they would have greatly exaggerated figures that were open to all.

Philadelphia was the scene of perhaps the hottest contest over the election of delegates that occurred anywhere. The city had at that time a population of about 28,000 inhabitants. At the election, the candidate who stood the highest at the polls, George Latimer, received 1215 votes while his leading opponent received only 235 votes. Thus a total of 1450 votes was cast in the election—about 5 per cent of the population.

The total population of the state in 1790 was 434,373, and allowing for the difficulty of journeying to the polls in the rural districts, it seems that the estimate of the dissenters was probably not far from correct.

It appears that in Baltimore 1347 voters participated in the election of representatives from that city. McHenry at the head of the poll received 962 votes and it was known that he favored unconditional ratification of the Constitution. His leading opponent received 385 votes. This vote was taken after a considerable demonstration, for a newspaper report says that "On the same day, the ship builders, the tradesmen concerned in navigation, the merchants, the manufacturers and several thousand inhabitants walked in procession through the different streets of the town." Baltimore had at that time a population of 13,000 so that a very large proportion of the adult males took part in the election.

Further light is thrown on the vote in Maryland by an opponent of ratification in a long paper printed in the Maryland Journal of May 16, 1788, signed "Republican." The author, says [Bernard C.] Steiner, "asserts that the 'common class' of people knew little of the Constitution. The two thousand copies of that document printed by order of the Assembly were too few to go far. The Annapolis paper is of small circulation, and the two Baltimore ones are never seen on the Eastern Shore, while the severe weather during the past winter prevented any newspapers from being sent over thither. Of the 25,000 voters in the state, only 6000 voted at the election and 4,000 of these votes were cast in Baltimore town and seven of the counties. The rich and wealthy worked for the Constitution to prevent the loss of their debts, and in some counties the opposition had named no candidates."

In South Carolina, the distribution of representation in the convention was such as to give a decided preponderance to the personalty districts along the sea-board. The convention of 1788 was composed of approximately twice the number of the house of representatives in 1794 and the apportionment was similar in character. In the latter year, R. G. Harper, under the pen-name of "Appius" pointed out the great disparity in the weight of the upper and lower districts in the legislature: "The lower country, including the three districts of Charleston, Beaufort, and Georgetown [which were strongly in favor of ratification of the Constitution], contains 28,694 white inhabitants, and it elects seventy representatives and twenty senators. Divide 149,596, the whole number in the state, by 28,694, those of the lower country, and the result will be more than five, from whence it appears, that a large majority of both branches of the legislature is elected by less than one-fifth of the people." The upper district [largely Anti-Federal], on the other hand, contained 120,902 white inhabitants, and sent only fifty-four members to the house of representatives. On this basis, the seventy-three votes cast in the convention against ratification may in fact have represented a majority of the white inhabitants and voters in the state.

While one hesitates to generalize about the vote cast in favor of the Constitution

on the basis of the fragmentary evidence available, it seems worth while, nevertheless, to put together several related facts bearing on the matter.

In addition to the conclusion, brought out by Dr. Jameson, that about 5 per cent of the population voted in Massachusetts in the period under consideration, we have other valuable data. Dr. Paullin has shown that the electoral vote in the presidential election of 1788 in New Hampshire was 2.8 per cent of the free population; that the vote in Madison's electoral district in Virginia in the same election was 2.7 per cent of the white population; that the vote in the first congressional election in Maryland was 3.6 per cent of the white population and that the vote in the same congressional election in Massachusetts was 3 per cent. Speaking of the exercise of the franchise as a whole in the period, Dr. Paullin says, "The voting was done chiefly by a small minority of interested property holders, a disproportionate share of whom in the northern states resided in the towns, and the wealthier and more talented of whom like a closed corporation controlled politics."

In view of these figures, in view of the data given above on the election of delegates (to the ratifying conventions) in the cities of Boston, Philadelphia, and Baltimore, in view of the fact that the percentage participating in the country was smaller than in the towns, and in view of the fact that only 3 per cent of the population resided in cities of over 8000, it seems a safe guess to say that not more than 5 per cent of the population in general, or in round numbers, 160,000 voters, expressed an opinion one way or another on the Constitution. In other words, it is highly probable that not more than one-fourth or one-fifth of the adult white males took part in the election of delegates to the state conventions. If anything, this estimate is high.

Now in four of the states, New Hampshire, Massachusetts, New York, and Virginia, the conventions at the time of their election were either opposed to the ratification of the Constitution or so closely divided that it was hard to tell which way the final vote would go. These four states, with Rhode Island and North Carolina, which were at first against ratification, possessed about three-fifths of the population—in round numbers 1,900,000 out of 3,200,000 free persons. Of the 1,900,000 population in these states we may, with justice it seems, set off at least 900,000, that is, 45,000 voters as representing the opposition. Add to these the voters in Pennsylvania who opposed the ratification of the Constitution, approximately 6000, and we have 51,000 dissenting voters, against ratification. Adding the dissenters in Maryland, South Carolina, and Connecticut, and taking the other states as unanimous, we may reasonably conjecture that of the estimated 160,000 who voted in the election of delegates, not more than 100,000 men favored the adoption of the Constitution at the time it was put into effect— about one in six of the adult males.

Admitting that these figures are rough guesses, it appears, nevertheless, that the Constitution was not "an expression of the clear and deliberate will of the whole people," nor of a majority of the adult males, nor at the outside of one-fifth of them.

Indeed, it may very well be that a majority of those who voted were against the adoption of the Constitution as it then stood. Such a conjecture can be based on the frank statement of no less an authority than the great Chief Justice Marshall who took a prominent part in the movement which led to the formation and ratification of the new instrument of government.

At all events, the disfranchisement of the masses through property qualifications and ignorance and apathy contributed largely to the facility with which the personalty-interest representatives carried the day. The latter were alert everywhere, for they knew, not as a matter of theory, but as a practical matter of dollars and cents, the value of the new Constitution. They were well informed. They were conscious of the identity of their interests. They were well organized. They knew for weeks in advance, even before the Constitution was sent to the states for ratification, what the real nature of the contest was. They resided for the most part in the towns, or the more thickly populated areas, and they could marshall their forces quickly and effectively. They had also the advantage of appealing to all discontented persons who exist in large numbers in every society and are ever anxious for betterment through some change in political machinery.

Talent, wealth, and professional abilities were, generally speaking, on the side of the Constitutionalists. The money to be spent in the campaign of education was on their side also; and it was spent in considerable sums for pamphleteering, organizing parades and demonstrations, and engaging the interest of the press. A small percentage of the enormous gain to come through the appreciation of securities alone would have financed no mean campaign for those days.

The opposition on the other hand suffered from the difficulties connected with getting a backwoods vote out to the town and county elections. This involved sometimes long journeys in bad weather, for it will be remembered that the elections were held in the late fall and winter. There were no such immediate personal gains to be made through the defeat of the Constitution, as were to be made by the security holders on the other side. It was true the debtors knew that they would probably have to settle their accounts in full and the small farmers were aware that taxes would have to be paid to discharge the national debt if the Constitution was adopted; and the debtors everywhere waged war against the Constitution —of this there is plenty of evidence. But they had no money to carry on their campaign; they were poor and uninfluential—the strongest battalions were not on their side. The wonder is that they came so near defeating the Constitution at the polls. . . .

Three conclusions seem warranted by the data presented in this chapter ["The Economics of the Vote on the Constitution"]:

Inasmuch as the movement for the ratification of the Constitution centred particularly in the regions in which mercantile, manufacturing, security, and personalty interests generally had their greatest strength, it is impossible to escape the conclusion that holders of personalty saw in the new government a strength and defence to their advantage.

Inasmuch as so many leaders in the movement for ratification were large security holders, and inasmuch as securities constituted such a large proportion of personalty, this economic interest must have formed a very considerable dynamic element, if not the preponderating element, in bringing about the adoption of the new system.

The state conventions do not seem to have been more "disinterested" than the Philadelphia convention; but in fact the leading champions of the new government appear to have been, for the most part, men of the same practical type, with actual economic advantages at stake.

The opposition to the Constitution almost uniformly came from the agricultural regions, and from the areas in which debtors had been formulating paper money and other depreciatory schemes. . . .

At the close of this long and arid survey—partaking of the nature of catalogue —it seems worth while to bring together the important conclusions for political science which the data presented appear to warrant.

The movement for the Constitution of the United States was originated and carried through principally by four groups of personalty interests which had been adversely affected under the Articles of Confederation: money, public securities, manufactures, and trade and shipping.

The first firm steps toward the formation of the Constitution were taken by a small and active group of men immediately interested through their personal possessions in the outcome of their labors.

No popular vote was taken directly or indirectly on the proposition to call the Convention which drafted the Constitution.

A large propertyless mass was, under the prevailing suffrage qualifications, excluded at the outset from participation (through representatives) in the work of framing the Constitution.

The members of the Philadelphia Convention which drafted the Constitution were, with a few exceptions, immediately, directly, and personally interested in, and derived economic advantages from, the establishment of the new system.

The Constitution was essentially an economic document based upon the concept that the fundamental private rights of property are anterior to government and morally beyond the reach of popular majorities.

The major portion of the members of the Convention are on record as recognizing the claim of property to a special and defensive position in the Constitution.

In the ratification of the Constitution, about three-fourths of the adult males failed to vote on the question, having abstained from the elections at which delegates to the state conventions were chosen, either on account of their indifference or their disfranchisement by property qualifications.

The Constitution was ratified by a vote of probably not more than one-sixth of the adult males.

It is questionable whether a majority of the voters participating in the elections for the state conventions in New York, Massachusetts, New Hampshire, Virginia, and South Carolina, actually approved the ratification of the Constitution.

The leaders who supported the Constitution in the ratifying conventions represented the same economic groups as the members of the Philadelphia Convention; and in a large number of instances they were also directly and personally interested in the outcome of their efforts.

In the ratification, it became manifest that the line of cleavage for and against the Constitution was between substantial personalty interests on the one hand and the small farming and debtor interests on the other.

The Constitution was not created by "the whole people" as the jurists have said; neither was it created by "the states" as Southern nullifiers long contended; but it was the work of a consolidated group whose interests knew no state boundaries and were truly national in their scope.

ROBERT E. THOMAS (1921–) is Vice-Chancellor of Educational Communications of the State University of New York. In this selection Thomas has examined several indices of economic and social status in Virginia with an eye to testing the accuracy of Charles Beard's depiction of that state's hard-fought ratification contest. Beard had seen the Virginia contest as one between the wealthy personalty holders of eastern Virginia and the small farmers and debtors of the western part of the state. After assessing the significance of his data, Mr. Thomas argues that there was no great clash of economic interests between the Federalist and Antifederalist leaders, but rather that they were both drawn from the gentry of their respective sections. Thomas concludes by labeling the conflict in Virginia as only sectional. Before accepting this selection's conclusion, the student should ask himself whether any sectional conflict can be completely free of economic differences, that is, whether the existence of a sectional conflict is not at least partial confirmation of Beard's thesis in Virginia.*

Robert E. Thomas

An Economic Interpretation Tested and Found Wanting

Perhaps no other book in the past half century has aroused more controversy than Charles A. Beard's *Economic Interpretation of the Constitution of the United States* (New York, 1913). Yet in spite of the debate which has raged about Beard's thesis and despite its susceptibility to empiric test, few writers have set about to determine inductively whether the poor were generally Anti-Federalists and the rich for the most part Federalists. This essay, a study of the economic and social status of the members of the Virginia state ratifying convention of 1788, is an attempt to answer this question so far as it applies to Virginia.

In his section on Virginia in the chapter entitled "The Economics of the Vote on the Constitution" Beard, drawing heavily on the works of Orin G. Libby** and Charles H. Ambler,† demonstrates

---

**Orin G. Libby, *The Geographical Distribution of the Vote of the Thirteen States on the Federal Constitution, 1787–8* (Madison, Wis., 1894).

†Charles H. Ambler, *Sectionalism in Virginia* (Chicago, 1910).

---

*Reprinted by permission of the Managing Editor from Robert E. Thomas, "The Virginia Convention of 1788: A Criticism of Beard's *An Economic Interpretation of the Constitution*," *Journal of Southern History*, XIX, No. 1 (February, 1953), 63–72. Most footnotes omitted.

that the vote on the Constitution corresponds rather closely to the four geographical sections within Virginia at that time—the Tidewater, the Piedmont, the Great Valley, and in the far western part of the state, Kentucky. Beard believed that the Tidewater, which was "almost solid in favor of ratifying the Constitution," supported the new government because here were concentrated the greatest number of large slave and landowners, as well as the heaviest concentration of commercial interests; that the Piedmont, which "was largely against ratifying the Constitution," voted as it did because in this region there were fewer personalty interests and a higher percentage of small farming debtors; that the vote of the Great Valley, which was overwhelmingly in favor of the federal government, "has not yet been traced to economic reasons"; and that the Kentucky district, which "was almost solid against ratification of the Constitution," opposed the new government because of the "frontier economic characteristics of the region" (that is, absence of personalty interests) and "the question of the opening of the Mississippi river." Implicit in this picture of the vote on the Constitution is a political contest between the rich and the poor. The rich, because of their excessive numbers in the East,* won that region for the Federalists; the poor, because of their preponderance in the West, aligned that region with the Anti-Federalists.

Beard's thesis, however, rests upon no other foundation than Libby's demonstration that the conflict in Virginia was

sectional. But to suggest that this was a class conflict because the East—where were concentrated the greatest number of personalty interests—voted for the Constitution, while the West—where was concentrated the highest percentage of small farming debtors—voted against it, overlooks the fact that there were personalty interests in both sections, and that there were small farming debtors in the Tidewater as well as in the West. The question of whether the conflict in Virginia was class as well as sectional depends upon whether the personalty interests in both sections voted as a unit in favor of the Constitution, and whether the debtors in both sections voted against it. Definitive proof of the nature of the contest in Virginia awaits an exhaustive study of "all" the personnel involved. In the meantime the data here presented offer substantial proof that the leaders of both the Federalist and Anti-Federalist parties came from the *same* class—slaveowners, large landowners, land speculators, army officers and professional people, in short, the gentry—and that the conflict, for whatever reasons, was only sectional.

Because of the absence of extensive commercial interests in Virginia during this period (in 1790, only 18,539 persons out of a total population of over 700,000 lived in Virginia's nine principal towns) the most extensive personalty was in slaves. Thus any test of the Beardian thesis must concern itself largely with an investigation of the ownership of slaves. Was a substantial majority of Virginia's approximately 290,000 slaves owned by those who voted to support the new government, were they more or less equally divided between the two parties, or did the weight of Virginia's most extensive personalty lie with the Anti-Federalists? Unfortunately since the

---

* The "East" is here taken to mean the Tidewater, which voted for the Constitution, while the "West" designates the Piedmont and Kentucky, which opposed the Constitution. In a criticism of Beard's thesis the Great Valley may be forgotten, because Beard himself admitted that the vote of this region could not be traced to economic reasons.

returns for Virginia in the first United States census have been almost totally destroyed, no comparison of the holdings of individual members of both parties can be made from this source. However, the white and slave populations by counties have been preserved, and on the basis of a statewide comparison of all the counties it will be seen, from the chart below, that the greatest number of slaves, both absolutely and relative to the number of whites, was in the *Anti-Federalist* counties:

	ANTI-FEDERALIST	FEDERALIST	DIVIDED
Total Number of Whites	176,255	214,986	50,876
Total Number of Slaves	133,155	123,692	35,780
Ratio of Slaves to Whites	0.8	0.6	0.7
Total Number of Counties	35	39	10
Average Slaves per County	3,804	3,171	3,578

It would appear at first glance that the Federalists were by far the poorest in personalty of the three groups above. But this is true only on a state-wide basis. The lower figures (except population) for the Federalists results from the fact that fourteen Federalist counties, lying in or near the Great Valley, with a combined population of 99,890 whites, held only 13,483 slaves: a ratio of .1 slaves to each white. Caroline, a Federalist, Tidewater county, alone held 10,292 slaves, while its white population was only 6,994: a ratio of 1.4 slaves to each white. Thus the Great Valley, whose vote Beard says "has not yet been traced to economic reasons," distorts the Federalist figures for the rest of the state. A better indication of the relative wealth of the Federalists and Anti-Federalists, so far as Beard's thesis is concerned, may be had by a comparison of those Federalist and Anti-Federalist counties which did not lie in either the Federalist Great Valley or the Anti-Federalist southwestern part of the state. The twenty-five remaining Federalist counties, clustered for the most part in the Tidewater, contained 115,096 whites and 110,209 slaves: a ratio of .95 slaves per white. The twenty-five remaining Anti-

Federalist counties, which lay generally in the Piedmont, contained 146,196 whites and 129,253 slaves: a ratio of .88 slaves per white.

The conclusion suggested by the above figures is that—whether one views the state as a whole, in which case the Anti-Federalists appear somewhat richer in slaves than the Federalists, or contrasts only the Tidewater and the Piedmont, in which case the Federalists have absolutely fewer, but relatively slightly more slaves than the Anti-Federalists—the slaveholders did not, as a group, support the Federal Constitution. Instead, in the regions where slaves were most widely held, the slaveholders appear to have been more or less equally divided on the issue.

Yet however suggestive the above figures may be, they do not reveal the wealth of individual men who voted to adopt or to reject the Constitution. It is only when county and sectional lines have been breached, and the status of individual men who voted either for or against the Constitution has been determined, that the "economic interpretation" will have been adequately tested. The materials for such a study, unlike those for a county study, are extremely fragmentary; yet the chart which follows offers strong evidence that men owning substantially the same number of slaves were equally divided on the matter of adopting or rejecting the Federal Constitution:

SLAVES HELD BY INDIVIDUAL MEMBERS OF THE VIRGINIA CONVENTION

ANTI-FEDERALISTS		FEDERALISTS	
NO. OF OWNERS	NO. OF SLAVES OWNED	NO. OF OWNERS	NO. OF SLAVES OWNED
2	4	1	5
1	6	2	8
1	8	1	9
3	10	1	10
1	13	1	12
1	17	4	15
1	19	2	19
3	21	1	25
1	23	1	26
1	27	1	27
1	30	1	28
1	32	1	31
1	35	1	37
1	38	1	38
1	39	1	43
1	124	1	58
1	150	1	62
1	300	1	63
		1	88
		1	143
		1	200

Total number of slaves: 962
Total number of owners: 23
Average per owner: 42
Median: 21
(No specific figures for 55 Anti-Federalist delegates)

Total number of slaves: 1,019
Total number of owners: 26
Average per owner: 39
Median: 25.5
(No specific figures for 63 Federalist delegates)

In order to heighten the significance of the above figures the following tables are included. They may help to make

clearer what constituted a large, medium and small slaveholder, and to place the above delegates in their proper light.

It will be seen from the tables for Princess Anne, a Tidewater county, Prince Edward, a Piedmont county, and Hampshire, a western county, that anyone owning 15 slaves or more might be considered a large slaveholder for any of these regions. Of the eight Anti-Federalist delegates who owned fewer than 15 slaves two were from western counties, where, in view of the fact that 88 per cent of the heads of families in Hampshire, a western county, held no slaves at all in 1782, it is evident that anyone owning any slaves could be considered one of the wealthier men in that region. Of these western delegates, one, Alexander Robertson, from Mercer County, owned 10 slaves, and may thus be considered a man of extreme wealth for that county; another, Henry Pawling, from Lincoln County, owned 4 slaves, and was consequently a man of some wealth. Two other Anti-Federalists who owned fewer than 15 slaves were Joseph Haden, who owned 8, and Samuel Richardson, who owned 4, both from Fluvanna County. In 1782, 47 per cent of the heads of families in that county held no slaves, while of those who did own slaves 46 per cent owned less than 4, and only 11 per cent owned 8 or more. Thus Haden, with 8 slaves, may be considered one of the larger slaveholders in that county, while Richardson, who owned 4, may be considered one of that county's medium slaveholders. Of the remaining Anti-Federalists who appear above as owning fewer than 15 slaves, one, Joseph Jones, from Dinwiddie, a Piedmont county, owned 10 slaves, and may be considered a medium slaveholder for that region. Another, Jonathan Patteson, from Lunen-

PRINCESS ANNE COUNTY (Federalist, Tidewater) 1783 48% of the heads of families owned no slaves.		PRINCE EDWARD COUNTY (Anti-Federalist, Piedmont) 1783 37% of the heads of families owned no slaves.		HAMPSHIRE COUNTY (Western County) 1782 88% of the heads of families owned no slaves.	
NO. OF OWNERS	NO. OF SLAVES OWNED	NO. OF OWNERS	NO. OF SLAVES OWNED	NO. OF OWNERS	NO. OF SLAVES OWNED
98	1	15	1	56	1
60	2	19	2	30	2
53	3	16	3	22	3
34	4	13	4	7	4
29	5	12	5	3	5
26	6	10	6	8	6
25	7	8	7	6	7
9	8	7	8	1	8
9	9	8	9	3	9
10	10	5	10	5	10
13	11	4	11	4	12
7	12	4	12	1	13
6	13	5	13	1	15
7	14	2	15	1	16
7	15	4	16	1	21
5	16	4	17		
6	17	3	18		
4	18	4	19		
3	19	4	20		
4	20	1	22		
3	21	1	25		
2	22	1	28		
1	23	1	29		
2	24	1	30		
1	25	1	33		
1	28	1	34		
1	29	1	35		
1	30	1	43		
1	31	1	46		
1	47	1	64		
1	53				
1	72				

Total number of slaves: 2,656

Total number of owners: 431

Average per owner: 6.2

Total number of slaves: 1,468

Total number of owners: 158

Average per owner: 9.2

Total number of slaves: 513

Total number of owners: 149

Average per owner: 3.4

burg, a Piedmont county, owned 6 slaves in 1769; it may be presumed that his slave-holdings were somewhat larger by the time of the ratifying convention in 1788. Another, David Bell, from Buckingham, a Piedmont county, is listed as owning 13 slaves. This figure represents only those slaves which he inherited from his father-in-law, Henry Cary. It is nearly certain that his total holdings in slaves were considerably higher than this figure indicates. Finally, Theodorick Bland doubtless owned more than the 10 slaves for which he is listed above. This figure represents only those slaves which he owned in Amelia County, and not those which he is certain to have owned in his home county, Prince George, whose records have been destroyed.

Of the six Federalists above who owned fewer than 15 slaves, three were from western counties: Ralph Humphreys, from Hampshire, who owned 10 slaves, Thomas Lewis, from Rockingham, who owned 8, and Alexander White, from Frederick, who owned 9. All of these western delegates were large slaveholders for their region. Of the remaining Federalists who owned fewer than 15 slaves, one, Thomas Matthews was from the borough of Norfolk. Although the schedules for the heads of families in the first census have been destroyed, this census indicates that there were 1,604 whites in Norfolk borough in 1790 and 1,294 slaves: a ratio of .8 slaves per white. Matthews, who owned 12 slaves, was doubtless among the larger slaveholders in that borough. Another of these delegates was Charles Simms, from Fairfax, a Tidewater county, who owned 8 slaves. In 1782, 48 per cent of the heads of families in that county owned no slaves, and of those who did, 77 per cent owned less than 8. Simms may thus be considered of the upper-

middle slaveholding class in that county. Finally, James Johnson, from Isle of Wight, a Tidewater county, owned 5 slaves. Forty-four per cent of the heads of families in that county owned no slaves in 1782, and of those who did, 53 per cent held less than 5. Johnson, then, may be considered as belonging to the county's lower-middle slaveholding class.

From the tables and analysis above three conclusions seem warranted: first, a substantial majority of the delegates were among Virginia's largest slave-holders; second, those delegates who appear in the table above as owning fewer than 15 slaves were generally large slave-holders for their particular county; and third, there is no significant difference in the number of slaves held by those who supported and those who opposed the Constitution.

Also pertinent to a test of the "economic interpretation" is the position taken on ratification by men who had been officers in the Revolution. Virginia's army officers received for their military service enormous grants of western land. "For instance the basic award for a Major was 5,333 acres; for a Captain, 4,000 acres; for Lieutenants, Ensigns, Cornets, Midshipmen, Surgeon's Mates and Gunners in the Artillery, 2,666 acres. Privates and non-commissioned officers received from 100 to 200 acres. The awards to Generals, Colonels, and Lieutenant Colonels varied, some of them receiving more than 10,000 acres. Army officers, then, constituted a group with extensive holdings in western land. According to Beard, "the weakness of the Confederation, the lack of proper military forces, the uncertainty as to the frontiers kept the values of . . . large sections of the West at an abnormally low price." Consequently, those with large interests in western real estate "fore-saw the benefits which might be expected from a new and stable government" and voted in favor of the Constitution. While it may be true that the army officers voted as a bloc in other states, there was no such unanimity among the officers in Virginia.

ARMY OFFICERS	ANTI-FEDERALISTS	FEDERALISTS
General	1	2
Colonel	23	19
Lt. Colonel	3	5
Major	4	3
Captain	10	13
Lieutenant	5	4
Ensign	2	0
Surgeon's Mate	0	1
Sergeant	0	1
Rank Unknown	2	6
	Total: 50	Total: 54
Members of the Cincinnati	10	8

In comparing these figures, and it must be remembered that there were eleven more Federalists than Anti-Federalists, it is evident that the army officers were not, as a group, "in favor of the new Con-stitution." Instead, and despite their holdings in western land, it appears that about half of Virginia's officers voted against the Federal Constitution.

Also worth comparing is the number of professional people who appear in each party. There were, of course, more towns in the Tidewater than in the Anti-Federalist regions of the state, and it would be reasonable to expect somewhat more lawyers, doctors, and ministers among the Federalists than among the Anti-Federalists. While this is true, the slight difference in the number of pro-fessional people who appear in the two parties suggests that the members of this group voted as Federalists in the Tide-water and as Anti-Federalists in the Piedmont; that they voted, that is, accord-ing to region rather than class:

	ANTI-FEDERALIST	FEDERALIST
Lawyers	8	13
Doctors	2	3
Ministers	1	0

From the tables above it seems clear that "In the ratification . . . the line of cleavage for and against the Constitution was [*not*] between substantial personalty interests on the one hand and the small farming and debtor interests on the other." Instead, the leaders of both parties were recruited from the same class, and the contest over ratification of the Federal Constitution in Virginia was essentially a struggle between competing groups within the aristocracy.

STUART BRUCHEY (1917–) is Allen Nevins
Professor of American Economic History at Columbia
University; E. JAMES FERGUSON (1917–) is
Professor of American History at Queens College,
CUNY. In his critical review of Ferguson's *The Power
of the Purse*, Bruchey sees Ferguson as explaining the
1780s as a political victory of minority property
interests over the agrarian majority. Bruchey regards
such economic motivation as an inadequate explanation
for the Constitution. Ferguson answers that everyone
who sees economic forces as significant in history
cannot fairly be termed a follower of Beard. Also,
economic motives can be fitted into general attitudes.
Nevertheless, the problems that were felt most keenly
by the Federalists and which moved them to action
were ones involving social and economic interests.*

Stuart Bruchey
E. James Ferguson

The Constitution: A Result
of Social and Economic Interests

E. James Ferguson's *The Power of the
Purse: A History of American Public
Finance, 1776–1790* (Chapel Hill, 1961)
requires examination on two levels of
significance. A product of more than a
decade of research in primary sources,
it is, in the first place, a minutely informed financial history of the years
1776–90. The analyses of the composition
and growth of the public (federal) debt
excel anything in print. The long chapter
on speculation in that debt adds depth
and detail to our knowledge of that subject. But Ferguson's book is also an essay
in historical interpretation. As such, it
must also be examined from the point of
view of its contribution to the controversy
over the validity of Charles Beard's conviction that the interests of men of
property, especially investors in public
and state debts, provided the main motive
power behind the movement which
culminated in the adoption of the Constitution. Professor Ferguson seems
clearly to prefer disengaging his book
from that controversy, for he acknowledges near the end of it that neither the
Constitution nor the circumstances
leading to its adoption "are wholly
explained by the train of events and

*Reprinted by permission from Stuart Bruchey and E. James Ferguson, "The Forces Behind the Consti-
tution: A Critical Review of the Framework of *The Power of the Purse* [With a Reply by the Author]," *The
William and Mary Quarterly*, 3 s., XIX, No. 3 (July, 1962), 429–438. Most footnotes omitted.

35

conditions discussed here." I think it fair to say, however, that in the body of his book Ferguson makes every effort to explain the coming of the Constitution in terms of the economic and fiscal facts he discusses. Most serious readers, therefore, will relate the book to the growing literature of the Beardian controversy, to which Robert E. Brown, Forrest McDonald, Jackson T. Main, and Lee Benson have also made recent contributions.

Ferguson approaches the financial history of the Revolution and Confederation in terms of a series of contrasts. All of them grow out of what would appear to be his most fundamental conviction, namely, that the "broadest cleavage in American society was that which ranged mercantile capitalists and their allies against agrarians both great and small." The agrarian mode of public finance was "state-oriented," and "based on the issue and redemption of paper." Originating in colonial period techniques of discharging public debts "by levying heavy taxes payable in the certificates of indebtedness themselves," this was the familiar and popular mode, expressive of the will of the majority. With this mode Ferguson associates representative institutions and civil rights. Had the depreciated public debt originating in the Revolutionary War been distributed among the states, the bulk of it would probably have been retired by some such "cheap" method as levying taxes payable in securities.

Opposed to the "agrarian majority," however, was the "propertied minority," the mode of which Ferguson denotes as "high finance." Aware, as for that matter the leaders of the majority were also aware, of the intimate relationship between economics and politics, the aristocratic minority knew well that an undischarged federal debt would require that Congress be given powers of taxation in order to provide revenue for interest payments. This "power of the purse," they also knew, would make the central government, rather than the states, sovereign. For if the states absorbed and paid off the debt "Congress would have been left with depleted functions and little reason to claim enlarged powers. Creditors would have attached themselves to the states, and no ingredients would have remained to attract the propertied classes to the central government." What the minority wanted above all was a strong central government, one that would foster business enterprise, encourage the growth of "commercial capitalism," and rid the country of paper money, tender laws, price regulations, embargoes, and antimonopoly laws. It therefore wanted the central government rather than the states to have the obligation of paying off the debt, and it wanted the debt discharged in full (at par) and in specie. Having no use for democracy, the aristocratic minority pursued tactics akin to the ways of "European despotism."

Within this framework of analysis and values Professor Ferguson traces the fiscal and related political developments of the 1780's. Under the leadership of Robert Morris, the "Nationalists" of 1780–84 induced Congress to adopt as an addition to the public debt (loan certificates) the unredeemed obligations of the Commissary and Quartermaster Departments, and, as well, sums due the Continental Army. But because of its impecuniousness, Congress had to halt interest payments on the debt in 1780 and 1782. Several states proceeded to assume the obligation of both principal and interest payments, however, and with this tendency to decentralize the debt the nationalist movement subsided. It had mainly represented a faction within the middle states. What regalvanized and spread the geographic area of the movement were the excessive paper money issues of the mid-eighties and Shays' Rebellion. Conservatives everywhere envisaged a rising popular attack upon property. Thus, "Fear of social radicalism drove New England merchants and southern planters into alignment with middle state conservatives in support of the movement for the Constitution." After its adoption Hamilton merely adapted to prevailing circumstances the substance of Robert Morris's earlier proposals for the handling of the debt.

Professor Ferguson thus analyzes the forces behind the Constitution in terms of the political goals of minority property interests. In this sense his thesis may be said to affirm that of Charles Beard. But Ferguson prefers to occupy somewhat higher ground. He acknowledges that one cannot be precise about the relationship between securities holdings and political attitudes. While he is convinced that securities holders as a group supported the Constitution, he emphasizes the changing constituency of the group and the continuity of speculation throughout the 1780's.

In his summary discussion Ferguson expresses the view that Beard overstated the importance of economic motivation. I also think Beard did so, but I am unable to find any discussion of alternative forces in Ferguson's book. Like McDonald, who places economic motivation within the framework of conditions and prospects in varying states, Ferguson cannot divest his analysis of its economic substance. It is certainly impossible to ignore the presence of economic interest. Like Mt. Everest, it is there; and as with Everest the essential problem is one of scaling.

Professor Brown succeeds in convicting Beard of distorting Madison's Tenth Federalist, but that document does continue to provide contemporary evidence of the importance of economic considerations. As Ferguson well says, "To eliminate entirely the role of economic motive in the political affairs of the time is as doctrinaire and as unnecessary as Beard's overstatement of it."

Yet economic motivation is not enough. Ferguson exhibits its insufficiency quite clearly, I think, in the weakness of his explanation of the absence of serious division among "either the people or their delegates in Congress" over Hamilton's proposals for handling the public debt. How indeed can one explain this phenomenon if it is true that (a) "The broadest cleavage in American society was that which ranged mercantile capitalists and their allies against agrarians both great and small," and (b) Viewed from "the arch of the emerging Federalist system," Hamilton's specific proposals were "partisan, partial to wealth, commercial capitalism, the north as against the south, and denotative of the extremism which begat political parties"? Here we have broad social cleavage honed sharp by partisan proposals, yet without either Congress or people being "seriously divided" over them! Is it satisfactory to explain this lack of division in terms of the ineffectual efforts of an "undermanned" opposition? I think not. Indeed, the validity of the class analysis might well be reexamined in the light of the phenomenon of an undermanned opposition.

An even larger part of a more comprehensive explanation may inhere in the character of nationalism during the 1780's. The economic nature of Ferguson's subject may dispose him to too narrow an interpretation of the nature of the nationalist movement of that decade. While Morris and middle-states business interests probably played leading parts in initiating the movement, it may be that other and noneconomic events and forces operated to swell its ranks. Among these should be considered the psychological effects of victory by colonies over their powerful mother country, of continued occupation of the Lake posts by the British, and of seizures of American ships and sailors by the North African pirate states. David Ramsay's contemporary history of the American Revolution is a neglected source for an imposing variety of motives inducing both men and states to support the constitutional movement.

The prospects of increased employment for shipping, and the enlargement of Commerce, weighed with those States which abounded in sailors and ships, and also with seaport towns, to advocate the adoption of the new system; but those States or parts of States, which depended chiefly on agriculture, were afraid that zeal for encouraging an American marine, by narrowing the grounds of competition among foreigners for purchasing and carrying their produce, would lessen their profits. Some of this description therefore conceived that they had a local interest in refusing the new system. Individuals who had great influence in state legislatures, or who held profitable places under them, were unwilling to adopt a government which, by diminishing the power of the states, would eventually diminish their own importance: others who looked forward to seats in the general government, or for offices under its authority, had the same interested reason for supporting its adoption. Some from jealousy of liberty, were afraid of giving too much power to their rulers; others, from an honest ambition to aggrandize their country, were for paving the way to national greatness by melting down the separate States into a national mass. The former feared the New Constitution; the latter gloried in it.

Almost every passion which could agitate the human breast, interested States and individuals for and against the adoption of the proposed plan of government. Some whole classes of people were in its favor. The mass of public creditors expected payment of their debts from the establishment of an efficient government, and were therefore decidedly for its adoption. Such as lived on salaries, and those who, being clear of debt, wished for a fixed medium of circulation and the free course of law, were the friends of a constitution which prohibited the issuing of paper money and all interference between debtor and creditor. In addition to these, the great body of independent men, who saw the necessity of an energetic general government, and who, from the jarring interests of the different States, could not foresee any probability of getting a better one than was proposed, gave their support to what the federal convention had projected, and their influence effected its establishment.*

In his emphasis on the key role of "independent men" Ramsay sounds a melodic line which may historically deserve to stand above the dissonance. Many of these men, I suspect, were animated by an essentially nonpersonal concern over the viability of the fledgling Republic. Many wished to enhance its military security and promote its economic development. In addition, just as threadbare patience and pent-up anger played prominent parts in the nationalism preceding the War of 1812, weakness and the desire for dignity may have moved key minds in the crucial 1780's. At any rate, there would seem to be significant matter here for further investigation. What might well be more closely examined are the interpenetrating effects of nationalism, social structure, and expanding economic opportunity.

*Ramsay, *History of the American Revolution*, (Philadelphia, 1789), II, 342–343.

E. James Ferguson's Rebuttal

Mr. Bruchey in his perceptive analysis puts *The Power of the Purse* on the pro side of the controversy over Beard. So does Richard B. Morris in his recent article, "Class Struggle and the American Revolution," *William and Mary Quarterly*, 3d Ser., XIX (1962), 3–29. This categorization is especially interesting to me, because other reviewers have classed me with the revisionists who are finally laying Beard's ghost.

My understanding of the book is that is does not support Beard at several crucial points. The treatment of state assumption of federal securities during the Confederation might be employed to cast doubt on the unity of the creditor interest. The role of public creditors in the adoption of the Constitution is projected far below the implications of the Beard thesis. According to several reviewers, Hamiltonian funding is described in terms downright favorable to Hamilton. I might add that in some ways the book sustains the distinctly old-fashioned notion that the Confederation was a critical period.

But I see Mr. Bruchey's point. The book incorporates the idea that there were differences in attitudes and interests between commerce and agriculture, between big property and small property, and among social classes, which led to political divisions, and that the classes of the nation possessing higher status and property were the driving force behind the movement for the Constitution. My initial reply to Mr. Bruchey would be that these concepts are not Beard's alone; that his work is not the sole test of their validity; that they infuse the sources for the period and constitute the operative hypotheses of a good many historical studies of it, old and new; and that subscribing to them does not necessarily make one a Beardian, unless indeed the name is given to anyone who deals with social and economic divisions as major causal factors.

This last point seems to be the heart of the matter. Beard has become a symbol of two generations of Progressive and socialist-oriented historical writing in the United States. The current revisionism is a reaction against that school. It has supplied a valuable corrective and has greatly refined historical interpretation of the period. It is sometimes overstimulated, however, by the impulse to assert the unity of American society in the face of the Communist challenge. Revisionist scholars working in Beard's field have honestly plied their craft, but both outside and inside the profession some of the enthusiasm engendered by their work seems to stem from the hope of banishing social conflict and economic motive from our history altogether.

The Power of the Purse was written neither to refute Beard nor to uphold him. Although several of its governing concepts are related to the Beard thesis, they are in other ways quite independent of it. The overriding theme is the interpretation of constitutional history in the context of public finance. Since the power to tax was fundamental to sovereignty, relations between Congress and the states hinged upon the location of the taxing power and hence upon details of financial policy and debt payment. Such issues pointed up the antagonism between advocates of centralized authority and adherents to the system established under the Articles of Confederation. Until 1787 the nationalist cause was represented by the effort to vest the Revolutionary debt in Congress and give Congress the taxing power to support it. But public finance was state-oriented during the Confederation and worked in a contrary direction. The issue was resolved by Congress's acquisition of taxing power under the Constitution and by the adoption of Hamilton's funding program, which implemented the new form of government by funding the debt.

Viewed in these terms, the evolution of government in the United States becomes an extension of English parliamentary development. The principles involved go back to the privilege of medieval parliaments, the struggle against the Stuarts, the opposition of colonial lower houses to British governors, and the resistance to Britain that culminated in the American Revolution. Until 1790 the constitutional history of the United States follows a continuous tradition.

The thesis of the book can be stated so far without reference to the composition of forces on either side of the constitutional issue, but with the analysis of interests and motives it gets into the area of the Beard controversy. Currency finance methods inherited from colonial times are linked with state sovereignty, the libertarian Whig philosophy of the Revolution, and agrarian values. The nationalists are described in terms of conservative, propertied, and mercantile interests; their political goals are shown to be interwoven with economic ends, particularly the establishment of a nationwide regime of sound money and contractual obligation.

These aspects of the book have been well formulated by Mr. Bruchey, and I will try to answer the legitimate questions he has raised. I gather that he has no serious quarrel with my delineation of fiscal and economic matters; his question is whether they are sufficient to account for the Constitution and the policy acts

of the new federal government. He alludes, instead, to national exhilaration inspired by victory in the war, desire for national dignity, and disinterested concern for national security. As proof that economic issues did not seriously disturb this high degree of unity, he cites my statement that Hamilton's proposals for funding the public debt aroused no great opposition.

As to the last point, the explanation is simply that the argument over funding the federal debt was settled by 1790. The issue had been resolved by the adoption of the Constitution. Funding was instrumental to the powers and functions of the new government; without funding, constitutional revision would have been inoperative. The predominance of Federalists in the new government and the conservative nature of its support virtually ensured that the mode of funding would be "high finance" rather than the agrarian methods of the past. There was little protest to Hamilton's formula because there was no practical alternative that would not undermine the union, and men of property, whether of the mercantile or landed interest, were singularly united over its preservation. In an age of upper-class stewardship it was their opinion that was politically effective. Although a broad division of interest existed between agriculture and mercantile capitalism—which revived soon after the Union was founded—it was submerged during the Constitution-making period in a general upper-class desire for strong government and economic reform. I have always thought, in this connection, that Beard's attempt to divide the aristocracy at this time according to real and personalty interests was untenable.

As to Mr. Bruchey's cavil about a interpretation couched solely in terms of economic motive, it is perfectly sound, if economic motive is construed in terms of crass interest like the ownership of securities or the desire to evade payment of debt. The reorganization of the governmental system after 1787 was an event on too grand a scale to be explained in such terms. But economic motives may be broadly conceptualized, embodied in general attitudes, and clothed with values. In the argument over Beard his detractors usually argue the narrow definition, his defenders take the large one, and the debate gets muddy. But if the larger version is taken, and one may still call such motives economic, or perhaps social, I would argue that a good deal about the constitutional period can be explained in terms of such motives, infiltrated at times by aims of the crasser sort.

Since this book is on fiscal and economic matters, it does not dwell upon other factors that would have to be given due weight in a full-dimensional study of the Constitution. Certainly, there were independent men who were concerned about national security or alarmed at the prospect of disunion—which nobody viewed with any relish. A growing sense of nationalism provided an indispensable setting for constitutional revision. During and after the Revolution the American states showed a remarkable willingness, given their freedom of action, to co-operate with one another and accept the rulings of Congress. As the book relates, the movement for constitutional change took place in a country that already acquiesced in it; by 1786 all the states had agreed to give Congress limited taxing power and there was general consent to federal regulation of trade. It was the collapse of such efforts to strengthen Congress under the Articles of Confederation that impelled the states to send delegates to the Federal Convention and that made the work of the Convention possible.

But the Constitution cannot be explained primarily in terms of agreement upon the need for reform; it was not reform but a revolution in government that far exceeded previous desire and expectation. Nor, except in the minds of a few, did it spring from an abstract conception of a better form of government. In principle and by tradition the nation was opposed to strong central authority. The weakness of the Articles was not a defect but a virtue until its shortcomings became visible, not merely in its failure to achieve broad national purposes, upon which there was not always clear agreement, but in concrete instances which affected the immediate or prospective interests of individuals. Violation of property rights, unchecked majority rule, local insurrection, the inability of the government to foster trade or pay its debts—these were the grievances recited in Federalist literature and by the delegates to the Convention as their main reason for being there. The effort to cope with them is clearly apparent in specific clauses and in the general structure of the Constitution. From the extent of Anti-federalism it is evident that they were not felt by everyone in the same degree; the mere fact that they were a source of conflict betokens differences in interest and viewpoint. Admittedly, considerations of a general nature were involved that transcended any division over these issues. One need not impugn the ideas of the Founding Fathers as to the proper structure of good government. Many people not otherwise partisan must have been incensed by the inconstancies of state and federal policy under the Confederation. And although the presence of Britain and

Spain on our borders was not generally considered an immediate threat, any perceptive man must have been concerned with the ultimate danger of war or foreign intervention in a weak system of states. However, notwithstanding the influence of such general and psychological factors, I think that the specific nature of constitutional revision, the actual context in which it occurred, and the results that flowed from it are most adequately explained in terms of social and economic interests.

ORIN G. LIBBY (1864–1952) taught at the University
of North Dakota from 1902 to 1945, retiring in the
latter year with the rank of professor. His study was
the first to suggest a sectional division on the
Constitution, other than the free state–slave state split
mentioned by James Madison during the Philadelphia
Convention. Basing his research on voting records,
Libby painted the commercial areas of the country
as Federalist and the noncommercial areas, where
subsistence farming predominated, as Antifederalist.
Libby's findings were referred to by Beard as
reinforcing his conclusions. The student should
examine the question of whether the relatively broad
conclusions of Libby do not at least partially undercut
Beard's narrow definition of the vital force in the
formation of the Constitution.*

Orin G. Libby

The Influence of Geography
and Paper Money

Turning now from the economic and
social groupings within the state to the
interstate groupings, we find that they
not only cross state lines but are arranged with reference to physical geography into great social and economic
units. In New England the eastern belt
of the Federal area extends along the
coast with hardly a break from Maine
to New York, Rhode Island being the only
considerable interruption in its continuity. The Connecticut valley was
another Federal region and was the decisive one for the Constitution in New
Hampshire and Massachusetts, and was
very important in Connecticut. This
coast area and this river valley were the

oldest and consequently the richest and
most commercial regions of New England, and their combined influence
was able to secure the adoption of the
Constitution there.

The grouping of the opposition areas
in New England is also very significant.
It will be seen that from about Lake
Winnepesaukee southward through New
Hampshire, Massachusetts and Rhode
Island, the Anti-Federal area extends
with hardly a break, and it also reaches
into northern Connecticut, and west of
the Connecticut river and south of the
Merrimac in Massachusetts, forming the
great interior region of New England, the
part most remote from commercial cen-

*Reprinted by permission from Orin G. Libby, *The Geographical Distribution of the Vote of the Thir-
teen States on the Federal Constitution, 1787–8,* Bulletin of the University of Wisconsin, Economic, Political
Science and History Series, Vol. I, No. 1 (Madison: University of Wisconsin, 1894), 46–49, 50–52, 69. Footnotes
omitted.

ters, with interests consequently predominantly agricultural. This was the debtor and paper money region and one peculiarly sensitive to taxation. It included factious Rhode Island, the Shays region in Massachusetts and the center of a similar movement in New Hampshire. The coincidence of opposition areas will be noted also in eastern New Hampshire and southwestern Maine, and in northwestern Connecticut and southwestern Massachusetts. In the same way the Federal area of Connecticut will be seen to be coincident with Federal and divided regions in New York, and also that of New Jersey with the same state. From New Jersey southward along the coast the Federal area runs in a belt, widest at the north including all of New Jersey and Delaware, that part of Pennsylvania along the Delaware and Susquehanna rivers which may be called tide-water Pennsylvania, all that part of Maryland east of the Susquehanna and Chesapeake Bay, including Baltimore and Annapolis, tide-water Virginia and the adjoining portion of Maryland, northeastern North Carolina with Wilmington and Newbern, southeastern South Carolina and all of Georgia. This region, it will be noted, includes all the best harbors, all the great sea coast shipping ports, and the most densely populated and wealthiest portions of the middle and southern states and represents, therefore, a predominantly commercial interest. That portion of it in Virginia and North and South Carolina corresponds roughly with the region east of the fall line and geologically with the Tertiary area of the South. Parallel to this larger area lay two other Federal areas, the first including the Shenandoah Valley and adjoining counties, the second the valley of the Ohio river and its great tributaries. The first comprised York county, Pennsylvania,

the western part of Maryland, and the valley between the Alleghany and Blue Ridge Mountains still farther to the southwest. This valley was the most fertile in that section of the country. It was the line of the great Scotch-Irish and German migration into the South, and was the interstate highway for the produce of this whole interior region. Its population, largely Scotch-Irish and Germans from Pennsylvania, showed a peculiar independence and clear sightedness in their decision regarding the new constitution, voting not like the isolated land owners farther east, but as members of the commercial class whose interests were bound up in securing an efficient and centralized national government. The second of these western Federal areas lay along the Ohio river. It is less strongly marked and more broken than the other, because it lay on the frontier where peculiar and often conflicting interests tended rather to separate than to unite it to the east. This region extended from Pittsburgh to Louisville and is represented by west Northumberland county and Washington county in Pennsylvania, the western part of the West Virginia District of Virginia, and Jefferson county in the Kentucky district, and perhaps by Sumner county in Tennessee, on the Cumberland river.

We must not omit the city of Albany, at the head of the Hudson river navigation, a fur trade center of long standing and a point of distribution for produce to the south and of supplies to the west along the Mohawk, as well as a starting point for emigration into central New York. In North Carolina there were the interior towns of Halifax and Salisbury which were Federal in a large Anti-Federal district.

The opposition areas in New England have already been referred to. In New York this area seems for the most part isolated except on the southeast where it touches that of Massachusetts. In Pennsylvania the Anti-Federal area lies entirely surrounded, in the great interior highland of the state. In Virginia we come upon an opposition area that is broadly connected with that of North Carolina, Kentucky, South Carolina, and Tennessee. It is the great Anti-Federal area of the country, touching the sea only at scattered points in Virginia, and in North Carolina for nearly one half its coast line where harbors are almost lacking. It contained few harbors, it was less thickly settled and more interior in its ideas and interests. It was an economic and social unit, without reference to state lines, moved by common impulses, sharing common prejudices, alarmed by the same fears. One of the best illustrations of the effect of this sort of environment on a people is seen in the case of the Germans who settled in North Carolina from Pennsylvania. In the latter state the Germans supported the Constitution, in Maryland likewise, and when settled along the Shenandoah valley their votes were unitedly for the Constitution. But those who came into the interior of North Carolina, cut off from all outside interest, on no great commercial highway like the Susquehanna, the Delaware, or the Shenandoah Valley, became conservative, suspicious of new ideas, and were readily led by politicians into opposing what was really for their best interests. While those in Pennsylvania, Maryland, and West Virginia were the strongest supporters of the new constitution, those in North Carolina were its most obstinate enemies, and even in 1789, the only united opposition came from these German counties in central North Carolina.

To sum up, the Constitution was carried in the original thirteen states by the influence of those classes along the great highways of commerce, the sea-coast, the Connecticut river, the Shenandoah valley and the Ohio river; and in proportion as the material interests along these arteries of intercourse were advanced and strengthened, the Constitution was most readily received and most heartily supported. In other words, the areas of intercourse and wealth carried the constitution. It was these sections that Hamilton rallied to support his far-seeing financial policy for continued national development. And it was in the interior and agricultural sections of the country that Jefferson found material for a party to oppose his great rival.

As these commercial lines multiplied in number and importance the national idea became more and more dominant. But the initial conflict was fought out in the period of ratification.

One of the fundamental reasons for calling the Constitutional Convention of 1787 was a desire to provide for the public necessities a revenue adequate to the exigencies of the Union. Various attempts of the old congress to secure amendments to the Articles of Confederation having this end in view had been fruitless, on account of what Madison mentions as a reason for the refusal of Rhode Island to attend the convention at Philadelphia, namely: "An obdurate adherence to an advantage which her position gave her of taxing her neighbors through their consumption of imported supplies." Obviously, a relinquishment of this source of state revenue and a diversion of it to the uses of the Union meant for these states the imposition of internal taxes to make good the resulting deficiency. Such a proposition would be opposed by those regions which were averse to taxation in general. The deeply-rooted antipathy to systematic taxation felt by interior agricultural regions has been well shown by Professor Sumner in his biography of Alexander Hamilton. In his introduction to the debates in the convention, Madison says:

In the internal administration of the states, a violation of contracts had become familiar, in the form of depreciated paper made a legal tender, of property substituted for money, of installment laws, and of the occlusions of the courts of justice, although evident that all such interferences affected the rights of other states, relative to creditors, as well as citizens within the state. Among the defects which had been severely felt, was want of a uniformity in cases requiring it, as laws of naturalization and bankruptcy, a coercive authority operating on individuals, and a guaranty of the internal tranquility of the states.

In a letter of Madison to Edmund Randolph of Virginia, April 8, 1787, occurs the following:

Let it (the Federal government) have a negative, in all cases whatsoever, on the legislative acts of the states, as the king of Great Britain heretofore had. This I conceive to be essential, and the least possible abridgment of the state sovereignties. Without such a defensive power, every positive power that can be given on paper will be unavailing. It will also give internal stability to the states. There has been no moment, since the peace, at which the Federal assent would have been given to paper money.

At the outset of the Convention, Governor Randolph is reported as follows:

In speaking of the defects of the Confederation, he professed a high respect for its authors, and considered them as having done all that patriots could do, in the then infancy of the science of constitutions and of confederacies; when the inefficiency of requisitions was unknown—no commercial discord had arisen among any states—no rebellion had appeared in Massachusetts—foreign debts had not become urgent—the havoc of paper money had not been foreseen—treaties had not been violated; and perhaps nothing better could be obtained, from the jealousy of the states with regard to their sovereignty.

Such statements as these reveal the presence of a debtor party, whose opposition to the new constitution was to be expected, a party favoring paper money and stay and tender laws, and opposing added taxation. If the commercial classes were in favor of a constitution that promoted national credit, commercial intercourse, and the rights of the creditor, it is just as certain that one of the most important factors with which the historian of the period has to reckon was the existence of an opposition party which found its interests endangered by such constitutional provisions, as the clause forbidding the states to issue bills of credit or to make anything but gold and silver a tender for debts, and the clause forbidding the violation of the obligation of contracts. On the surface of the debates in the Constitutional Convention and in the ratification conventions of the various states, these issues do not appear so clearly as do controversies concerning the danger of the extension of the taxing power and respecting general abstract principles of liberty and state sovereignty. Nevertheless they were issues up for settlement, and the people felt themselves vitally concerned in the matter. Seven of the states had issued paper money between 1785 and 1786, and there was a paper money party in every one of the thirteen states at the time of the ratification of the Constitution. This party demanded not only paper money, but also stay and tender and debt laws of such a character as would, if enacted, defraud the creditor of his dues. The same spirit made itself felt in the resistance encountered in many of the state legislatures to passing the necessary legislation to give effect to the British treaty of 1783, especially as relates to the securing of British debts. And it was to be expected, that, wherever this party was found, there would be a center of opposition to the Constitution; since its ratification meant an end to paper-money issues and a strict enforcement of debts. . . .

In each of the original thirteen states that ratified the Constitution the testimony is of the same general character, confirming the original thesis stated at the beginning of the chapter. And it is not the least significant fact revealed in the evidence that in the three states ratifying unanimously in 1788, there was found to be a faction in favor of paper money corresponding in location and character to similar factions in the remainder of the states. Hamilton, in giving an enumeration of the factors in opposition to the new constitution mentions "the disinclination of the people to taxes, and of course to a strong government;

the opposition of all men much in debt, who will not wish to see a government established, one object of which is to restrain the means of cheating creditors."

It has been shown in previous chapters that the opposition to the Constitution was confined to those interior or sparsely settled districts that were the last to receive population, and whose interests were agricultural as opposed to commercial; rural as opposed to urban. It has been shown in this chapter that the factions in favor of paper money issues, and tender laws and opposed to the enforcement of the British treaty of 1783, were to be found in the great interior agricultural sections of the country, where the debtor class outnumbered the creditor, where taxes were unpopular and capital scarce. And finally the conclusion has been reached that these factions of 1785–6 were closely related to the Anti-Federalist party of 1788.

JACKSON TURNER MAIN (1917–   ) is Professor
of American History and Director of the Institute of
Colonial Studies at the State University of New York
at Stony Brook. Main modified Libby's conclusions
and included as supporters of the Constitution those
who participated in any way in the commercial life of
the nation. This helps to explain the considerable
support the Federalists received from city workers
whose prosperity usually depended directly on a
thriving commerce. Under Main's definition of
"commercial interest" farmers who produced crops for
sale, often for export, would also be included.*

Jackson Turner Main

Capitalism versus Agrarianism

If urban classes were not divided, was
there not a class division implicit in a
sectional alignment over the Constitution? This thesis, which was most fully
developed by Libby, set east versus west,
or, to be more accurate, seacoast versus
backcountry. Libby's protagonists were
the debtor areas of the interior and the
creditor, mercantile centers near the
coast. Emphasizing the issues which
separated the two general regions, he
stressed the correlation between Antifederalism and paper money as a proof
of his hypothesis.

This interpretation has much truth.
There had most certainly been just such
a division all during the colonial period,
and it continued to be of great importance
for many decades. There is an abundance
of evidence to support this explanation;
as a matter of fact, the contrast between
seacoast and interior was in some cases
even more marked than Libby believed.
The strength of Antifederalism was
greater in upstate New York and backcountry South Carolina than he appre-
ciated, and he did not fully exploit the
possibilities of Rhode Island or of Maine.
It is also true, as he contended, that
paper money was a factor in the contest.
In Massachusetts, towns opposing paper
were Federal by about four to one, while
pro-paper money towns were Antifederal
by an even wider margin. The hard (or

*Reprinted by permission from Jackson Turner Main, *The Antifederalists: Critics of the Constitution,
1781–1788* (Chapel Hill: University of North Carolina Press for the Institute of Early American History and
Culture, 1961), pp. 268–281. Footnotes omitted.

less soft) money towns in New Hampshire were Federal; most of the Antifederal strength in Connecticut was found in paper money districts; and the case of Rhode Island is sufficiently familiar. In New York it was the Clinton party which favored bills of credit in 1784, 1785, and 1786. Delegates from the Federal counties of New York, Kings, and Richmond had voted against such issues; and when Suffolk and Queens counties finally changed sides and voted for ratification, they joined long-time allies on the paper money question. The same was true of the individuals involved: New York's Federalists had opposed paper money, whereas Antifederal members of the convention had voted for it, twenty-one to eleven; of the eleven Antifederalists who had opposed paper money, no less than seven were among those who ultimately changed sides on the Constitution or refrained from voting. Thus the advocates of hard money drew together in support of the Constitution. In Maryland and in Virginia the paper money forces opposed ratification. This was also the case in North Carolina, while in South Carolina, Antifederal strength lay in the backcountry, which had favored inflation.

All of the foregoing, however, does not prove an exact correlation between Antifederalism and the advocacy of paper money. There are a large number of exceptions, and of course there is a limit to the number which may be admitted without invalidating a rule. Leaving aside the fact that many Antifederalists, especially the leaders, specifically denounced state currency emissions, we have to consider the following exceptions: (1) in South Carolina, a large number of planters, most of whom became Federalists, supported the state's paper emission; (2) most Antifederalists in Virginia (including the planters) were opposed to paper money; (3) in Maryland, according to Crowl, attitudes toward paper money are not the key to the situation, and indeed the correlation with opinions on the Constitution is certainly not high; (4) New Jersey endorsed both paper money and the Constitution; (5) in Pennsylvania, although it is probable that a majority of the people were Federal, a majority favored paper money; (6) in Connecticut, paper money sentiment was far stronger than Antifederalism. Other exceptions could be cited.

That paper money sentiment was in some degree a factor in the existence of Antifederalism is scarcely to be doubted —the Antifederalists drew more heavily by far than their opponents from the ranks of paper money advocates; however the correlation is by no means complete. A different approach is necessary if all, or even most, of the facts are to be explained, and the real causes for the alignment understood. It will be necessary first to examine the positions taken by the different social or economic groups.

Among the groups into which the population might conceivably be divided, there were some whose members did not take a consistent stand on the Constitution. It has already been observed that religious and racial groups insofar as they voted together seldom did so for reasons connected with religion or race. Speculators in western lands varied in their attitude toward the Constitution; their votes were determined by local factors or personal interest. Members of the "intelligentsia," if such a thing existed then—the writers, teachers, artists, and the like—were divided almost equally; doctors showed a slight but indecisive tendency toward Federalism.

Merchants, on the other hand, were virtually unanimous in endorsing the

Constitution. It would not be quite accurate to say that every one of them supported ratification, but at least 80 per cent of them were Federal. It did not matter where they were located—in Boston or in Savannah, Pittsburgh, or Alexandria—nor what their economic status was, they were Federal almost to a man. In addition all, or very nearly all, of those who were immediately dependent upon commercial activities held similar views. This was the "Mercantile Interest" which, as John Adams once defined it, included "Merchants, Mechanicks, Labourers." Understood in this way, the world takes in important segments of the population, including shipowners, seamen and other persons in maritime industries, the "mechanics and artisans," the apprentices and other hired employees in almost every town, and all those who depended upon any of the above. But the commercial interest was not just urban. The commercial centers were supported by nearby rural areas which depended upon the towns as markets and as agencies through which their produce was exported overseas. That is to say, the commercial interest also embraced large numbers of farmers, and the influence of each town radiated, perhaps in a degree relative to its size or commercial significance. The same influence permeated the rich river valleys and bound the great planters and other large landowners in the commercial nexus. Just as in physics each point along a beam of light itself acts as a point source of light, so also the major channels of commerce, rivers or roads, influenced the country through which they passed. The mercantile interest, understood in this broad sense, is the key to the political history of the period. Its counterpart is the non-commercial interest of the subsistence farmer. This is a socioeconimic division based on a geographical location and sustains a class as well as a sectional interpretation of the struggle over the Constitution.

A brief review of the evidence will make clear the importance of this generalization. In Maine, the seacoast towns, dependent on the export of fish or lumber, favored ratification by a margin of over two to one, while the largely self-sufficient towns of the interior were Antifederal. The towns along the Connecticut River favored ratification. This was true in Connecticut, Massachusetts (with a few exceptions in the northern part of the state), New Hampshire, and possibly Vermont, where the southeastern counties became Federalist strongholds. The situation in Rhode Island is also striking. At first Federal strength was probably limited to four towns, all on the coast, including the only important commercial centers. Three other towns which may have been Federal in 1788 were also coastal. In 1790 all of the towns which supported the Constitution were with two exceptions on the coast. From Narragansett Bay, the center of commercial activity, Federalist strength gradually reached out into the adjacent hinterland. In New England, then, the major division was between the areas, or people, who depended on commerce, and those who were largely self-sufficient. That the distinction was recognized at the time is shown by the observations of the residents of Spencer (Worcester County) who referred to their town as one of those whose "Distent Situation, from the metropolis ... Renders the profits, of ... farmes, Very Inconsiderable, to Those, of an equal Bigness, and Quality, near, the Maritime And, market Towns."

In New York and in the remaining states the data cannot be quite so precise because the political unit was the county rather than the town, and it is therefore more difficult to distinguish the commercial from the non-commercial interest. The Federalism of the towns, however, is obvious and has been sufficiently discussed. The Federalism of the countryside surrounding New York City is also to be noted; so too is the remark of Thomas Tredwell that the contest was "between navigating and non-navigating individuals." Spaulding notes the opposition of merchants and non-merchants and observes that "the Clintonians were scarcely interested in commerce," while Cochran defines the Antifederalists as farmers "who had no direct interest in trade or commerce."

The vote in Pennsylvania is also significant. Counties which had immediate access to the Delaware (Philadelphia, Bucks, Northampton) or which were but a score of miles distant (Montgomery and Chester) together with the counties adjoining the lower Susquehanna (Lancaster and York) cast thirty-seven votes for and only one against the Constitution, whereas the remainder of the state cast twenty-two votes against and nine for ratification. George Bryan believed that an important feature of the division was the fact that men of trade and their supporters were Federal; he contrasted the counties near to and remote from "the navigation" and observed of the mechanics, "such as depend on commerce and navigation, in favor." John Armstrong found that Antifederalism was dominant among the "country people." New Jersey and Delaware do not quite fit this, or any other pattern, although it might be noted that both were favorably situated for supplying domestic and foreign markets. In Maryland the only Antifederal support came from the country; the location of the state between the Chesapeake and the Potomac may be compared with that of the Northern Neck

between the Potomac and the Rappahannock.

In assessing the situation in Virginia, it is illuminating to consider the vote in 1785 granting commercial powers to Congress. Although it is not quite a straightforward test of the commercial and non-commercial interests, yet the correlation between the alignment on this issue and that on the Constitution is striking. The Federalist counties (including the "Alleghany" region) favored the measure by a margin of over two to one, while Antifederal counties rejected it by nearly three to one. It is true that there were few merchants or commercial towns in the state, but the great planters were essentially commercial farmers who recognized that their future depended on trade, and it is no accident that Virginians took the lead in the effort to bestow the commerce power on Congress. On the other hand large parts of the state were further from the trade routes, so that many people either had nothing directly to do with commerce or did not recognize any identity of interest with the mercantile community. It has already been noted that the division within the state was fundamentally that of the river valleys versus the non-valley areas. The vast majority of counties which bordered the major streams were Federal, whereas Antifederal strength lay principally in the regions more distant from such waterways, notably in the Southside.

The fact that North Carolina contained a large proportion of subsistence farmers certainly was instrumental in shaping its Antifederalism. Evidence has already been adduced which indicates that the planters in the southeastern portion of the state, in spite of their greater wealth, had on several issues been opposed to the merchants, whereas the northeastern planters had voted on the other side.

It is significant that the Constitution's sole support came from the Albemarle Sound counties and from the towns.

Still farther south, the foreign trade of South Carolina had always been of fundamental importance, symbolized by the interrelationship of planter and merchant in Charleston; all along the coast the producers of rice, indigo, and forest products voted with the city. On the southern border, the Savannah River drew inhabitants of both banks into the Federal camp, for not only did South Carolinians dwell under its influence but nearly the entire state of Georgia was at this time contained within the single river valley.

In all parts of the country, therefore, the commercial interest with its ramifications, including those who depended primarily and directly upon commerce, were Federal, and the "non-navigating" folk were Antifederal.

The mercantile interest drew many groups into its orbit. Manufacturers were with few exceptions comprehended within the term "artisans and mechanics." They were skilled workers with a small shop or master craftsmen with a few apprentices. Such men either depended directly upon overseas trade, producing goods for export (coopers, sailmakers, and dozens of others) or sold their products to those who were merchants or closely associated with merchants. In addition it is well known that they hoped for protection against British competition. They are therefore to be included as part of the commercial interest, and their very livelihood seemed to them to depend upon the adoption of the Constitution. Few of these men were chosen to the ratifying conventions, but many voted, or expressed their opinion in less formal ways (as in Boston), and their attitude is clear. In addition there were some,

though not yet many, who owned fairly large establishments. A number of these men—upwards of a dozen—did attend the conventions and were Federalists with but one or two exceptions. Other businessmen were also dependent upon commerce. The majority—indeed nearly 70 per cent—of the lawyers and judges favored ratification. When they lived in non-commercial areas, such as in parts of Virginia, they were Antifederal, or where peculiar circumstances existed the usual condition might be changed: in North Carolina the lawyers (Federal) and judges (Antifederal) had been previously opposed, while in New York the Clintonian party contained its share of both. Judgeship or a law practice in itself did not determine political belief, but it did predispose the individual to act in concert with those of equal status or similar economic interest.

With regard to the creditors of the federal government the situation is somewhat different. The whole question of the debt is a very complex one, but some tentative observations may be made. It is almost certainly true that most of the debt was held by Federalists, for the certificates were concentrated in the more wealthy and the urban areas. It does not require more than a superficial examination of the records to secure the evidence of this. Three different groups may be distinguished. First, there were those holding public securities who lived in states which were paying the interest in a fairly satisfactory manner. These men, in their capacity as security holders, would not be vitally affected by the Constitution unless they feared a local change of policy. Second, there were those owning certificates who lived in states which were not paying the interest in a satisfactory manner. These men would gain heavily by the ratification. Third, there were those who held no securities. The last two need further discussion.

The mere fact that a person held securities did not mean that he favored ratification. Most of the creditors owned too small amounts to constitute a vital interest. In Virginia, although about a third of the members of the ratifying convention subscribed to the loan of 1790, only a handful had $1,000 in securities. Fully 85 per cent of the delegates either had no securities or their holdings were too small to have constituted a motivating factor. Six of the large holders, moreover, were Antifederal. Presumably these men can be exempted from the imputation of economic motive, and in the case of certain other known creditors it is evident that other considerations governed their decision: Isaac Vanmeter, a West Virginian; Archibald Stuart of the Shenandoah Valley; John Marshall; and Edmund Randolph. When all the facts are considered, it becomes evident that the personal holdings of the delegates were not an important factor in shaping their political convictions. Similarly, in Pennsylvania only nine members of the convention held large amounts; four of them were Antifederal. In New York security holders were at first more numerous among Antifederal than Federal delegates to the convention, but it is instructive to note that about half of the Antifederal security holders were among those who changed sides on the final vote. Only seven of those who had securities held large amounts; four of these were chosen as Antifederalists, and three of the four changed sides.

It seems clear that of the approximately three hundred members of the conventions in these three important states, not over 10 per cent could have been persuaded to favor ratification because of the public securities they held. It is true that outside of the conventions there were large security holders, and that a great deal of money was at stake, but it is evident that the public creditors comprised only one of many interests.

In regard to those who did not own public securities the situation is quite complex. It would be to their interest to keep the tax burden as low as possible, but in some cases the Constitution might actually be advantageous. McCormick argues convincingly that New Jersey favored ratification because the taxes for payment of the debt would be lowered. In other cases ratification would make little difference if taxes were already being levied for the purpose. In still other states the non-holders did stand to lose, and there were objections to the Constitution on that ground. The division certainly was not simply one of holder versus non-holder. A majority of the former favored ratification and a majority of the latter opposed it, but in neither case was the distribution of the debt at all decisive; probably, with some exceptions, it was not even very important compared with the influence of commercial factors.

The influence of private debts was undoubtedly very great. In the absence of extensive data concerning who owed whom, it is necessary to proceed by inference; this, however, may be done with some confidence. There were two major types of debtors: those who had fallen into debt because they were poor (typified by the small farmer), and those who had borrowed although they had considerable property (typified by Southern planters). Just as there is no strict dividing line between farmer and planter, so also one variety of debtor merges into the other; nevertheless a broad distinction exists. The different classes of debtors behaved differently. George Bryan remarked that in Pennsylvania debtors as a group did not agree on ratification, for, as he pointed out, "debtors are often creditors in their turn." Those who were engaged in business had to pay their debts promptly if they were to receive the further credits which were essential to them, and such men therefore held creditor views about "sound money" and "honesty in business." This category included most characteristically the merchants, but many, if not most, of the large landowners as well. In general, it seems that the class of what might be termed well-to-do debtors were divided in their attitude toward the Constitution, but that a majority of them were Federal. In South Carolina, measures benefiting debtors had found much support in the Federal eastern parishes; many Virginia planters who were in debt to British or American merchants were Federal; in Pennsylvania some prominent Republicans supported a paper money bill. In New York the Federalist Henry Remsen and other merchants petitioned for relief from debts due to British merchants. The Shenandoah Valley delegates were Federal, though at least six of them were well-to-do debtors. Another student has found that those owing money to British merchants were divided politically. It may be concluded that although some large property holders opposed the Constitution because of their debts, the majority were Federalists regardless.

The other type of debtor, typified by the small farmer, was numerically more important. The testimony of contemporaries, the number of court suits, and the passage of various laws demonstrate the prevalence of debtors in every state. The decided majority were in the Antifederal column. We have seen that advocates of paper money were apt to be Antifederalists; so also were those who favored other measures aiding debtors.

In South Carolina, for example, a valuation law, an instalment law, and a "Pine Barrens" law were supported by the western counties; the votes on such matters previously discussed reveal an alignment very similar to that on the Constitution, even including the uncertain stand of those parishes which changed sides. Benjamin Rush and Charles Pinckney both emphasized the importance of these issues. In Virginia the votes on bills concerning the British treaty are especially significant, as are those postponing taxes in 1783 and 1784. Similar correlations existed elsewhere: in North Carolina, New York, and all of the New England states. In general, then, creditors were usually to be found on the Federalist side; debtors, with many exceptions especially among the more well-to-do, were Antifederal. This fact confirms the generalizations that have been previously made concerning the alignment on ratification.

When a question so complex as the ratification of the Constitution is examined, it is to be expected that any generalization will be surrounded by exceptions. If too much attention is devoted to these exceptions, the generalization may become obscured or disguised, if not entirely hidden, so that one may even be mistaken for the other. On the other hand, if the over-all view is to be successfully maintained, and the generalization proved valid, the exceptions must be accounted for. In the case we are considering, it would be too much to contend that the division between commercial and non-commercial elements entirely accounts for the alignment over the Constitution, and even when it is added that a division along class lines is also evident, much remains unexplained.

Along the great arc of the frontier, for example, were two areas which were Federal because of their peculiar circumstances. These are, first, backcountry Georgia, which wanted protection from the Indians, and second, a region including West Virginia, the Shenandoah Valley, and western Pennsylvania, which hoped that a strong central government could drive out the British and Indians. In these areas, military and diplomatic considerations, rather than socio-economic factors, determined a preference for the Constitution. There were also several instances in which the influence of prominent local leaders brought Federalism to unlikely spots. Such was probably the case in northern New Hampshire, Huntingdon and Luzerne counties in Pennsylvania, and parts of Berkshire County in Massachusetts. Another exceptional instance is the strength of Federalism in the interior of Connecticut, which is especially surprising when contrasted with the Antifederalism of Rhode Island; the reasons are to be found in the quite different economic, political, and perhaps even cultural backgrounds of the two areas.

The magnitude of the Antifederalists' victory in New York and their quick defeat in Pennsylvania are equally puzzling; the Hudson was a great commercial highway which should have recruited strength for Federalism in the interior, whereas much of the Quaker state was backcountry and should have adhered to Antifederalism. Here the major explanation lies in contrasting political trends in the two states. In Pennsylvania, the conservative Republicans were increasing in strength, whereas in New York the Clintonian party had governed so successfully that it had never lost control. Special circumstances, like those we have already noted, governed the situation in other states, such as New Jersey, Delaware, and Maryland.

But after all of these facts have been taken into account, we can return to the major generalization: that the struggle over the ratification of the Constitution was primarily a contest between the commercial and the non-commercial elements in the population. This is the most significant fact, to which all else is elaboration, amplification, or exception. The Federalists included the merchants and the other town dwellers, farmers depending on the major cities, and those who produced a surplus for export. The Antifederalists were primarily those who were not so concerned with, or who did not recognize a dependence upon, the mercantile community and foreign markets. Such people were often isolated from the major paths of commerce and usually were less well-to-do because they produced only enough for their own purposes. Because of this basic situation, a majority of the large property holders were Federal, but this division along class lines did not exist in the towns and not everywhere in the country. It was real enough however to find reflections in the political ideas of both sides. Because the Federalists dominated the towns and the rich valleys, they included most of the public and private creditors, great landowners, lawyers and judges, manufacturers and shipowners, higher ranking civil and military officials, and college graduates. Although the Antifederalists derived their leadership from such men, the rank and file were men of moderate means, with little social prestige, farmers often in debt, obscure men for the most part.

Antifederal thought was shaped by the composition and objectives of the party, but was modified by the social and political attitudes of the articulate leaders through whom it was expressed. Only a few of these leaders came from the small farmers or truly represented them. They frequently defended views somewhat less democratic than those of their constituents, and they were often out of sympathy with the economic demands of the rank and file, especially in the case of paper money and debtor relief legislation. As a result, Antifederalism as formulated by its most prominent spokesmen sometimes lacks the democratic overtones we have attributed to it.

But the democratic implication existed. As a body of political thought, Antifederalism had a background in English and American political theory long before the Constitution was drafted. Its principles were embodied in the Articles of Confederation; later they were elaborated in the controversy over the impost. Always the emphasis was on local rule and the retention of power by the people, which were democratic tenets in that age. Such a body of thought could of course be used by special interest groups; its bare political doctrine was put forth in opposition to the impost by the merchants of Rhode Island and Massachusetts. But it was always more congenial to the many than the few. Throughout the 1780's, whenever the question of sovereignty arose, the same men representing the same interests rehearsed the arguments they were to employ in debating the Constitution. Although the Antifederalist position was employed to mask special interests, it was fundamentally anti-aristocratic; whoever used its arguments had to speak in terms which implied, if they did not clearly define, a democratic content. It was therefore peculiarly congenial to those who were tending toward democracy, most of whom were soon to rally around Jefferson. The Antifederalists, who lost their only major battle, are forgotten while the victors are remembered, but it is not so certain which is the more memorable.

STAUGHTON LYND (1929–   ) has taught at Yale
University, Spelman College, Atlanta, and Roosevelt
University, Chicago. He is currently with an anti-war
group, The Chicago Resistance. In the selection
presented here, Lynd argues that New York Federalists,
although led by a group of conservative aristocrats
intent upon regaining lost power in the state, were
strongly supported by New York City's working class,
who saw in the Constitution a possible defense against
lower priced foreign manufactures which were
threatening their livelihood. The aristocratic leaders
of the Federalist movement also had an economic
motive, in that they saw a stronger central government
as improving the foreign commerce of the United
States. The economic and political interests of the
Federalist leaders and their working class supporters
soon diverged, and they resumed their struggle for
control of the state. Although Lynd writes only of New
York, he implies that alliances of this sort may have
occurred in other cities. To Lynd, New York's case
shows that economic self-interest and democratic belief
were not invariably opposed to each other in the contest
for ratification of the Constitution. On occasion they
could cooperate on behalf of a document which affected
both economics and politics.*

Staughton Lynd

An Uneasy Alliance of Defensive
Aristocrats and Restless Mechanics

By silently consenting to the dichotomy
of economic self-interest and democratic
belief, [Beard's] critics have neglected
the possibility that the Constitution was
both capitalist *and* democratic, an "economic document" *as well as* a republican
manifesto to a revolutionary world.

I have argued elsewhere that the New
York Anti-Federalists embodied a similar
mixture of motives.* They were for the
most part "new men" of plebeian origin,
striving for equal access to economic
opportunity, social acceptance, and political leadership. But they were not

*"Who Should Rule at Home? Dutchess County,
New York, in the American Revolution," *William
and Mary Quarterly*, Third Series, Vol. XVIII
(1961), pp. 330–359.

*Reprinted by permission from Staughton Lynd, "Capitalism, Democracy and the United States Consti-
tution: The Case of New York," *Science & Society*, XXVII, No. 4 (Fall, 1963), 386–396, 402–405, 412–413. Most
footnotes omitted.

merely self-interested: for, resenting the pervasive domination of farm and forum by men of wealth and rank, they also genuinely sought to enlarge the number of people involved in the political process.*

The Federalists of New York exemplify even more dramatically the two-sided, ambiguous nature of the Revolutionary movement. Their brilliant leaders—Hamilton, Schuyler, Robert R. Livingston, Gouverneur Morris, Duane and Jay—*were* conservatives, and not merely in the revisionist sense that what they sought to conserve was liberal. They took it for granted that society was a hierarchy of ranks, with a wealthy and leisured elite at its head and "the lower orders" and "the peasants" under their rule. They were conservative also in the very modern sense of resisting fiercely government intrusions on free enterprise. Yet they were *also* deeply public-spirited men, critical of any tendency in each other to put private concerns before devotion to country and firmly committed to republican government.

As if the seemingly-contradictory qualities of the Federalist leadership were not confusing enough, the Federalist voters of middling and humble rank (to use the phrase then current) are even more puzzling. Beard dismissed the city

---

*Since the stress in the present essay falls on the Federalists rather than the Anti-Federalists, I take this opportunity to state that the Anti-Federalist leaders in New York City as well as in the countryside were for the most part "new men." The merchants who had been active in the Sons of Liberty before the Revolution became Federalists, with three exceptions, John Lamb, Marinus Willett, and Peter Curtenius, all of whom held important offices in the Clintonian administration (Isaac Sears, Alexander McDougall and John Morin Scott all died before the ratification struggle). New York City's Anti-Federalist leaders, typically, were merchants who came into the city at the end of the war, traded with the West Indies rather than with Europe, and did not belong to the New York Chamber of Commerce or attend Mrs. John Jay's dinner parties.

artisans as "politically non-existent," perhaps because their ardent support of the Constitution failed to fit his theory. But the nationalism of the mechanics—not only in New York, but every major city—needs to be explained. How was it that these vigorously democratic Sons of Liberty, whom the Lord of Livingston Manor called "restless mechanics" and Gouverneur Morris compared to a dangerous reptile, supported with enthusiasm a Constitution sponsored by patricians like Livingston and Morris? Why, after denouncing Hamilton as a tool of Tories and rich men in 1784, did the artisans turn about and idolize him in 1788 for pushing ratification through the New York state convention?

The following pages will document and attempt to clarify these paradoxes in the politics of New York ratification. The reader is asked to keep in mind the theoretical problem. To Beard it seemed obvious, by analogy to the robber barons of his own day, that if the Founding Fathers were substantial capitalists, concerned to fashion a society in which men of wealth and good family would have a decisive voice, then their professed devotion to popular government was hypocritical, and resistance to their rule by the mass of common men inevitable. It seemed obvious, but, as I hope to demonstrate, it was not true. The paradoxical reality was that this was a Constitution designed to promote capitalism, but defended by urban workingmen; a Constitution whose authors were avowedly fearful of democracy, but which established the most democratic government in any major nation of the world at that day.

The Federalist Leadership

Power in the State of New York before the American Revolution lodged in the hands of a small group of families whose income derived both from commerce and land. This was a ruling class, not merely in the sense that its members had similar interests, but also in the sense that they were bound together by close family ties (thus Hamilton married into the Schuylers, and Duane and Jay into the Manor Livingstons), shared a common ethos of *noblesse oblige,* and, at least in crises, tended to act together as a political unit. Beard's famous mistake (corrected in the second edition of his *Economic Interpretation*) of supposing that the Hudson Valley landlords opposed the Constitution, sprang from his over-narrow conception of economic interest, and in particular, from his artificial distinction between "realty" and "personalty." To which group did James Duane, proprietor of Duanesburg, kin to Livingstons, and Mayor of New York in the Critical Period, belong? Obviously to both. Chancellor Robert R. Livingston declared in 1780 that "I have no personal property," as his father had lamented eighteen years earlier that "my personall Estate is no more, and we ought to take care of the Reall." Alexander Hamilton, in contrast, was the principal spokesman of the nation's investors in fluid capital. Yet Livingston and Hamilton found common cause in the proposed United States Constitution and were the two principal Federalist speakers at the state ratifying convention.

What was at stake, in 1788, for both up-river landlords and metropolitan merchants, was aptly expressed in an exchange of letters between Alexander Hamilton and Robert Livingston, Jr. (the aged Lord of Livingston Manor) on the eve of the New York elections of 1785. "The situation of the State at this time is so critical," Hamilton wrote

that it is become a serious object of attention to those who are concerned for the *security*

of property or the prosperity of government, to endeavour to put men in the Legislature whose principles are not of the *levelling kind* [italics in original]. . . . All men of respectability, in the city, of whatever party, who have been witnesses of the despotism and iniquity of the Legislature, are convinced, that the principal people in the community must for their own defence, unite to overset the party I have alluded to. I wish you to be persuaded Sir, that I would not take the liberty to trouble you with these remarks with a view to serving any particular turn; but, from a thorough conviction, that the safety of all those who have anything to lose calls upon them to take care that the power of government is intrusted to proper hands.

After the election, Livingston replied:

In this last election, by compleating the necessary Junction previous to the day of Election [which] we have so often desired & Endeavourd for; by uniting the interests of the Rensselaer, Schuyler, & our family, with other Gentm. of property in the County in one Interest . . . we Carryed this last Election to a man.

"I trust," concluded the Third Lord, "we Shall always have the like Success provided we Stick Close to Each other."

In this illuminating exchange, property spoke to property, power to power, and the barriers separating proud great families and dividing city from country were overcome. The link between Hamilton and Livingston, as revealed by these letters, was surely basically economic: the political convictions on which they stood stemmed from a struggle for power between contending economic groups, and the power they sought meant economic security and dominion for their kind of people. Note that this is not economic interest in Beard's restricted sense of "advantages which the beneficiaries expected would accrue to themselves first" or an immediate interest in "personal possessions." That is what economic interest may mean in a stable society wherein legislation centers on the allocation of a pork barrel of discrete economic advantages among competing claimants. But the Constitution was the settlement of a revolution. What was at stake for Hamilton, Livingston, and their opponents, was more than speculative windfalls in securities: it was the question, what kind of society would emerge from revolution when the dust had settled, and on which group the political center of gravity would come to rest.

In 1788, in the State of New York, it was not at all certain which class would rule. However it may have been in other states, it was not true in New York that "leadership at the close of the [Revolutionary] era belonged substantially to the same segment of the society as it did at the beginning"; nor was it the case "that the social conventions governing the employment of the colonial franchise survived the Revolution without serious impairment." It was not true in Dutchess County, where landlords dropped out of politics after 1777, and not a single member of the old ruling families held important elective or appointive office until after 1788. It was not true in New York City, where the artisans fought bitterly in 1785 and 1786 for artisans in the legislature, and sought to make elective all important municipal offices from the mayoralty down. Nor was it true in New York State as a whole, governed throughout this period by a man whose "family and connections," in the words of his defeated opponent, did "not entitle him to so distinguished a predominance." Philip Schuyler, who said this about George Clinton, had boasted before the election of 1777, "they may chuse who they will I will command them all." It did not work out quite this way. Late in the war, Schuyler's son-in-law tactfully commented that the great man, then serving

in the New York Senate, was "exposed to the mortification of seeing important measures patronised by him frequently miscarry."

A strong anti-aristocratic spirit was at work among the common people of the state during the years 1777–1788, and in state politics, the little group of conservative nationalists was consistently on the defensive. When, in the spring of 1784, Robert R. Livingston acquired Oliver Delancey's "large square pew" at St. Paul's church, one might have thought the Revolution had been a personal success for him; but the triumph was tainted by the fact that in 1785, as in 1777, the Chancellor had to withdraw from the race for Governor "on account of the prejudices against his family name." Livingston himself was able to respond flexibly to the new times. Others were more impatient. On the eve of the Army-Congress plot of 1783, Morris wrote to John Jay (a passage omitted by Sparks from his version of the letter in his *Life of Morris*):

> You and I, my friend, know by Experience, that when a few Men of Sense and Spirit get together, and declare that they are the Authority, such few as are of a different Opinion may easily be convinced of their mistake by that powerful Argument the Halter.

The threat to upper-class power in Revolutionary New York was both economic and political. Underneath all political squabbles was the chronic discontent of tenant against landlord. The historian of the famous New York tenant revolt of 1766 remarked that "to what extent anti-rent agitation continued during the Revolution is difficult to say": the fact is that tenant troubles did continue and did seriously worry the patriot leaders. In Dutchess County, where some of the greatest landlords became Tories, tenants supported the Revolution in hopes of getting their land. Just north of Dutchess, in Columbia (now Albany) County, where the Livingston landlords were Whig, the tenants accordingly were strongly pro-British. In 1775, Robert R. Livingston (whose Clermont estate was the southern or "lower" portion of Livingston Manor) wrote to John Jay that his tenants had "resolved to stand by the King as they called it, in hopes that if he succeeded they should have their Lands"; the tenants, Livingston continued, had sent petitions of grievance to the Continental Congress which Jay should be sure to rebut, for they "will if they meet with the least encouragement throw the whole country into confusion." In May 1777, five hundred tenants on Livingston Manor, virtually its entire dependent population, rose in arms in support of the English troops descending from Canada with Burgoyne. Several men were killed and over three hundred rioters were imprisoned before the insurrection was put down.

The Livingston Manor rising was an index of the decay of aristocratic authority in Revolutionary New York. "We must think in Time," James Duane had written the Manor Lord two years before, "of the means of Assuring the Reins of Government when these Commotions shall subside." In May 1777, the reins were flapping loose. A distraught aunt summoned Philip Livingston home from the Continental Congress at Philadelphia; Peter Livingston made up packets of provisions should sudden flight prove necessary; the Lord of the Manor, their father, was advised by his sons not to leave the house. William Smith found Robert Livingston Jr. wildly inconsistent on every topic but one: "his Execrations upon his Tenants." "His Fears," Smith continued,

have driven him to Temerity. He exclaims agt. setting up any Governt. at this Juncture. . . . He says his Tenants owe him £10,000. He can't bare the thought that his Indulgences shew that he has no Influence upon them, much less that they are in such a Temper as to prevent him from riding about in his own Manor; and seeing no safety but in their Expulsion hints his wishes that they may be all hanged and their children starved.

It is easy to understand why Hamilton's appeal to this man for all those with something to lose to join forces against dangerous levellers, met such a ready response in 1785.

By 1783, however, the confiscation of Loyalist land had quieted the uproar among the tenants, and opposition to the nationalist party in the Critical Period took largely political form. By 1788, the Lord of Livingston Manor had so far recovered his position that a fellow-Federalist pleaded with him to "interpose his Authority" among the tenants to secure votes for ratification.

The political challenge to conservative power in New York came from aspiring new men like George Clinton, Abraham Yates, and Melancton Smith, figures who in many cases had begun their careers as stewards and surveyors for the great landed magnates whose power they now began to contest. In the first election under the new state constitution, in 1777, the old Son of Liberty John Morin Scott ran for governor along with Schuyler and Clinton, "rail [ed] at an *Aristocratic Faction* which he pretends has formed and organized the new government" and blamed his failure to obtain high office on Duer, Duane, Robert R. Livingston, Philip Livingston, and Gouverneur Morris, "whom he described as a faction & tends [sic] to a family interest." Defeated in the gubernatorial election, Scott used his Senate seat to introduce legislation for price-fixing and land confiscation. Gouverneur Morris commented on this radical program: "It was hardly possible to embitter [the] bitter Draught these Laws had prepared, yet it was effected by the manner of enforcing them. Men of old approved Character who respected their Neighbours and were respected would not descend to it. The Executors of these new Laws therefore were Men who like the Laws themselves were new." The Clintonian tax program, Hamilton agreed, was put into the hands of local assessors who used their power to punish Tories. Both in the legislature and in administration, "Men of Substance and Importance" (as the future Federalist, Egbert Benson, put it) dropped out of politics during the Revolutionary War. Into their shoes stepped such new men as Abraham Yates of Albany, whose rise was described by Schuyler as follows:

Abraham Yates, I mean the Honorable Abraham Yates Esq. one of the Senate of this State, a member of the Council of Appointment—one of the Committee of the City and County of Albany, Recorder of the City of Albany—& Postmaster General, late Cobler of Laws & Old Shoes, is to be put in Nomination for Lieut. Governor.

The tone of Schuyler's letter explains more about New York politics in the Revolution than volumes of statistics on "personalty" and "realty." At the 1788 ratifying convention, as George Dangerfield observes, the underlying antagonism between the old upper class and their plebeian antagonists was the actual substance of debate.

It was only as the New York conservatives lost control of state government to their upstart opponents, that the thought of the conservatives turned clearly in a centralist direction. At first, they were by no means the centralizing

nationalists which they later became. "I am resolved," Edward Rutledge wrote John Jay on the eve of the Declaration of Independence, "to vest the Congress with no more Power than that which is absolutely necessary, and to use a familiar Expression, to keep the Staff in our own Hands." This mood lasted just so long as the conservatives retained their confidence in controlling what Robert R. Livingston called the "torrent" of democratic sentiment in the states. When that confidence failed, when in 1779–1780 the conservatives turned to Congress to effect their program, they turned to it as "a refuge against majority rule." Hamilton wrote in July 1781 that "it would be the extreme of vanity in us not to be sensible, that we began this revolution with very vague and confined notions of the practical business of government." The remark applied as much to the future authors of *The Federalist* as to anyone else. . . .

The genuineness of artisan support for the Constitution is beyond question. The election for delegates to the New York ratifying convention was (as in no other state) by secret ballot and open to all adult males, and the New York City Federalist margin was twenty-to-one: since the artisans were a good half of the city's adult male population, they must have voted overwhelmingly for ratification. Moreover, as in all the other large cities, the city mechanics capped their ballots with a victory parade in which craft after craft marched under its banners.

As the artisan population of the city, three or four thousand strong, marched down Broadway on July 23, 1788, to celebrate adoption of the Constitution by the requisite nine states, their floats and slogans testified to their enthusiasm. A "federal loaf," 10 feet long, 27 inches in breadth, and 8 inches in height, was carried by the Bakers, together with "a flag, representing the declension of trade under the old Confederation." "Americans, encourage your manufactures!," proclaimed the Skinners, Breeches Makers and Glovers, while the Peruke Makers and Hairdressers rejoined, "May we succeed in our trade and the union protect us." The Blacksmiths chanted, "Forge me strong, finish me neat, I soon shall moor a Federal fleet," as sturdy members of the trade, riding the float, hammered away at an anchor. On they came—the Ship Joiners, with their motto: "This federal ship will our commerce revive, And merchants and shipwrights and joiners shall thrive"; the humble Cartmen, saying: "To every craft she gives employ, Sure Cartmen have their share of joy"; the Brush Makers, who proclaimed: "May love and unity support our trade, And keep out those who would our rights invade." And after these, there came several dozen more trades, including the Cordwainers, Carpenters (the largest trade, with 392 marchers), Hatters, Cabinet Makers, Sail Makers, Gold Smiths, Tobacconists, Paper Stainers, Artificial Florists, and last but not least the Tailors, with their magnificent slogan: "And they sewed fig leaves together."

Jackson Main has pointed up the theoretical significance of the artisans' Federalism. "The most serious of all objections to an interpretation based exclusively on an alignment along class lines," Main wrote, "is the complete absence of a division of opinion in the towns. Where there should have been the most feeling, the least existed." How shall we account for the artisans' enthusiasm for a document which, according to Beard, was the reactionary and antidemocratic product of a ruling class?

It will not do to explain away the Federalism of the artisans by observing that many of those termed "mechanics" in the eighteenth century were, in fact, property-owning small businessmen, more merchants than laborers. For the Jacobin mobs of Paris were also drawn from a variegated array of "workshop masters, craftsmen, wage-earners, shopkeepers, and petty traders," as were the supporters of John Wilkes in the out-parishes of London. Clearly what needs to be explained is why such groups were radical in contemporary Europe but conservative, at least in the sense of supporting a Constitution drafted by men of the wealthy upper class, in America.

The answer must go right back to John Fiske. The Federalist *leaders* knew what they wanted before 1783, but the New York City artisans, who would become Federalist *voters,* were preoccupied in 1783 and 1784 with a belligerent, class-conscious attempt to rewin a foothold in the city from which the war had exiled them seven years. The depression of the mid-1780's transformed their outlook. The spring of 1785 saw a general uneasiness about trade stagnation suddenly grow acute and urgent. Then, as John Jay remarked, Federal ideas began to thrive; the early summer of 1785 produced in every major American city a merchant-mechanic alliance on behalf of stronger Federal government.

The objects of the merchant-mechanic committees formed in Boston, New York, Philadelphia, Baltimore and Charleston in 1785 were, first, to press for stronger Federal power to regulate trade, and second, to reinforce legislation—as in Non-Importation days—by the moral sentiment and direct action of local communities. The first concern is illustrated by a petition from "Artificers, Tradesmen and Mechanics" of New York City to the

Continental Congress, early in 1785, which stated that "we sincerely hope our Representatives will coincide with the other States, in augmenting your power to every exigency of the Union." The second concern is exemplified by the resolve of the Philadelphia shoemakers not to buy, sell, repair, let be repaired by an employer, or work for employers who bought, sold or repaired, imported European boots or shoes.

Imported manufactures brought the menace of British economic power directly home to the New York City artisans. Thirty thousand hats and 97,000 pairs of shoes, for example, poured into the city during the three years 1784–1786. Here again was an echo of "the ever-memorable period of the Stamp-Act": after, as before, the Revolution, the encouragement of native manufactures seemed a part of the struggle for independence. "When the minds of the people of America were really virtuous," wrote a newspaper correspondent in 1785, "at the beginning of the late contest, every man was convinced of the necessity of our encouraging manufactures, and employing our own people, that we might be truly independent." . . .

The preceding pages have attempted to explain this startling alliance [of conservative gentry and city artisans]. The financial crisis of 1779–1780 crystallized the mercantilist, nationalist program of the Federalist leaders. The depression of 1785–1786 swung the city artisans behind this program, which seemed to them both a guarantee of economic expansion and a safeguard for American independence. Both groups felt an economic interest in the Constitution. To the conservatives it seemed to offer a check on the reckless interference with property by the states. To the artisans it offered jobs and markets. But for each group,

in addition, strengthening and consolidating the Federal government seemed a way to promote the Revolution. In the eyes of the artisan in the mid-1780's, as for the well-to-do conservatives in the "counter-revolutions" of 1780–1781 and 1787–1788, no contradiction existed between immediate, personal economic interests and the patriotic goal of sustaining the national economy and preserving national independence.

Unity on behalf of the Constitution was possible because both the conservative Federalist leadership, and its mechanic followers, sought to create a society which would establish representative government, and in which private property would be taken for granted. Fellow Whigs in New York were divided as to who should vote and as to whether elected representatives should be drawn from a limited social stratum; the artisans were more democratic, while the Federalist leaders are better described as republicans. But some form of representative government was a goal which no one questioned. A similar consensus of fundamentals existed regarding private property. The agitation of the artisans never went further than an expanding capitalist economy in which all might prosper. (The "levelling" tenants up-river, similarly, wanted nothing so much as farms of their own.) Merchants wanted a bank based on specie, while mechanics considered public emissions safer than any private bank; Alexander Hamilton wished to create government-chartered monopolies, Melancton Smith proposed (at the New York ratifying convention) to prohibit them. But the universal aim was to acquire property, not to abolish it. In economic as in political attitudes, patriotic New Yorkers differed within a broad framework of agreement.

STANLEY M. ELKINS (1927–   ) is Professor of
American History at Smith College; ERIC McKITRICK
(1919–   ) is Professor of American History at
Columbia University. In this essay the authors contrast
the relative youth and past record of national service of
the Federalists with the relative age and past record of
state service of the Antifederalists. These different
backgrounds led the "Young Men of the Revolution"
to turn to a nationalist remedy for the presumed ills of
the Confederation Congress and their opponents to
uphold state interests and power, even to the point
of rejecting the Constitution.*

Stanley M. Elkins
Eric McKitrick

Youth and Energy Carry the Day

Merrill Jensen has argued that the Federalists, by and large, were reluctant revolutionaries who had feared the consequences of a break with England and had joined the Revolution only when it was clear that independence was inevitable. The argument is plausible; few of the men most prominent later on as Federalists had been quite so hot for revolution in the very beginning as Patrick Henry and Samuel Adams. But this may not be altogether fair; Adams and Henry were already veteran political campaigners at the outbreak of hostilities, while the most vigorous of the future Federalists were still mere youngsters. The argument, indeed, could be turned entirely around: the source of Federalist, or nationalist, energy was not any "distaste" for the Revolution on these men's part, but rather their profound and growing involvement in it.

Much depends here on the way one pictures the Revolution. In the beginning it simply consisted of a number of state revolts loosely directed by the Continental Congress; and for many men, absorbed in their effort to preserve the independence of their own states, it never progressed much beyond that stage even in the face of invasion. But the Revolution had another aspect, one which developed with time and left a deep imprint on those connected with it, and this was its character as a continental war effort. If there is any one feature that most unites

*Reprinted by permission from Stanley Elkins and Eric McKitrick, "The Founding Fathers, Young Men of the Revolution," *Political Science Quarterly*, LXXVI, No. 2 (June, 1961), 202–216. Footnotes omitted.

the future leading supporters of the Constitution, it was their close engagement with this continental aspect of the Revolution. A remarkably large number of these someday Federalists were in the Continental Army, served as diplomats or key administrative officers of the Confederation government, or, as members of Congress, played leading rôles on those committees primarily responsible for the conduct of the war.

Merrill Jensen has compiled two lists, with nine names in each, of the men whom he considers to have been the leading spirits of the Federalists and Anti-Federalists respectively. It would be well to have a good look at this sample. The Federalists—Jensen calls them "nationalists"—were Robert Morris, John Jay, James Wilson, Alexander Hamilton, Henry Knox, James Duane, George Washington, James Madison, and Gouverneur Morris. Washington, Knox, and Hamilton were deeply involved in Continental military affairs; Robert Morris was Superintendent of Finance; Jay was president of the Continental Congress and minister plenipotentiary to Spain (he would later be appointed Secretary for Foreign Affairs); Wilson, Duane, and Gouverneur Morris were members of Congress, all three being active members of the war committees. The Anti-Federalist group presents a very different picture. It consisted of Samuel Adams, Patrick Henry, Richard Henry Lee, George Clinton, James Warren, Samuel Bryan, George Bryan, George Mason, and Elbridge Gerry. Only three of these—Gerry, Lee, and Adams—served in Congress, and the latter two fought consistently against any effort to give Congress executive powers. Their constant preoccupation was state sovereignty rather than national efficiency. Henry and Clinton were active war governors, concerned primarily with state rather than national problems, while Warren, Mason, and the two Bryans were essentially state politicians.

The age difference between these two groups is especially striking. The Federalists were on the average ten to twelve years younger than the Anti-Federalists. At the outbreak of the Revolution George Washington, at 44, was the oldest of the lot; six were under 35 and four were in their twenties. Of the Anti-Federalists, only three were under 40 in 1776, and one of these, Samuel Bryan, the son of George Bryan, was a boy of 16.

This age differential takes on a special significance when it is related to the career profiles of the men concerned. Nearly half of the Federalist group—Gouverneur Morris, Madison, Hamilton, and Knox—quite literally saw their careers launched in the Revolution. The remaining five—Washington, Jay, Duane, Wilson, and Robert Morris—though established in public affairs beforehand, became nationally known after 1776 and the wide public recognition which they subsequently achieved came first and foremost through their identification with the continental war effort. All of them had been united in an experience, and had formed commitments, which dissolved provincial boundaries; they had come to full public maturity in a setting which enabled ambition, public service, leadership, and self-fulfillment to be conceived, for each in his way, with a grandeur of scope unknown to any previous generation. The careers of the Anti-Federalists, on the other hand, were not only state-centered but—aside from those of Clinton, Gerry, and the young Bryan—rested heavily on events that preceded rather than followed 1776.

As exemplars of nationalist energy, two names in Professor Jensen's sample that come most readily to mind are those of Madison and Hamilton. The story of each shows a wonderfully pure line of consistency. James Madison, of an influential Virginia family but with no apparent career plans prior to 1774, assumed his first public rôle as a member of the Orange County Revolutionary Committee, of which his father was chairman. As a delegate from Orange County he went to the Virginia convention in 1776 and served on the committee that drafted Virginia's new constitution and bill of rights. He served in the Virginia Assembly in 1776 and 1777 but failed of re-election partly because he refused to treat his constituents to whisky. (He obviously did not have the right talents for a state politician.) In recognition of Madison's services, however, the Assembly elected him to the Governor's Council, where he served from 1778 to 1780. Patrick Henry was then Governor; the two men did not get on well and in time became bitter political enemies. At this period Madison's primary concern was with supplying and equipping the Continental Army, a concern not shared to his satisfaction by enough of his colleagues. It was then, too, that he had his first experience with finance and the problems of paper money. He was elected to the Continental Congress in 1780, and as a member of the Southern Committee was constantly preoccupied with the military operations of Nathanael Greene. The inefficiency and impotence of Congress pained him unbearably. The Virginia Assembly took a strong stand against federal taxation which Madison ignored, joining Hamilton in the unsuccessful effort to persuade the states to accept the impost of 1783. From the day he entered politics up to that time, the energies of James Madison were involved in continental rather than state problems—

problems of supply, enlistment, and finance—and at every point his chief difficulties came from state parochialism, selfishness, and lack of imagination. His nationalism was hardly accidental.

The career line of Alexander Hamilton, *mutatis mutandis,* is functionally interchangeable with that of James Madison. Ambitious, full of ability, but a young man of no family and no money, Hamilton arrived in New York from the provinces at the age of 17 and in only two years would be catapulted into a brilliant career by the Revolution. At 19 he became a highly effective pamphleteer while still a student at King's College, was captain of an artillery company at 21, serving with distinction in the New York and New Jersey campaigns, and in 1777 was invited to join Washington's staff as a lieutenant-colonel. He was quickly accepted by as brilliant and aristocratic a set of youths as could be found in the country. As a staff officer he became all too familiar with the endless difficulties of keeping the Continental Army in the field from 1777 to 1780. With his marriage to Elizabeth Schuyler in 1780 he was delightedly welcomed into one of New York's leading families, and his sage advice to his father-in-law and Robert Morris on matters of finance and paper money won him the reputation of a financial expert with men who knew an expert when they saw one. He had an independent command at Yorktown. He became Treasury representative in New York in 1781, was elected to Congress in 1782, and worked closely with Madison in the fruitless and discouraging effort to create a national revenue in the face of state particularism. In the summer of 1783 he quit in despair and went back to New York. Never once throughout all this period had Alexander Hamilton been involved in purely state affairs. His career had been a continental one, and as long as the state-centered George Clinton remained a power in New York, it was clear that this was the only kind that could have any real meaning for him. As with James Madison, Hamilton's nationalism was fully consistent with all the experience he had ever had in public life, experience whose sole meaning had been derived from the Revolution. The experience of the others—for instance that of John Jay and Henry Knox—had had much the same quality; Knox had moved from his bookstore to the command of Washington's artillery in little more than a year, while Jay's public career began with the agitation just prior to the Revolution and was a story of steady advancement in continental affairs from that time forward.

The logic of these careers, then, was in large measure tied to a chronology which did not apply in the same way to all the men in public life during the two decades of the 1770's and 1780's. A significant proportion of relative newcomers, with prospects initially modest, happened to have their careers opened up at a particular time and in such a way that their very public personalities came to be staked upon the national quality of the experience which had formed them. In a number of outstanding cases energy, initiative, talent, and ambition had combined with a conception of affairs which had grown immense in scope and promise by the close of the Revolution. There is every reason to think that a contraction of this scope, in the years that immediately followed, operated as a powerful challenge.

The stages through which the constitutional movement proceeded in the 1780's add up to a fascinating story in political management, marked by no little élan

and dash. That movement, viewed in the light of the Federalist leaders' commitment to the Revolution, raises some nice points as to who were the "conservatives" and who were the "radicals." The spirit of unity generated by the struggle for independence had, in the eyes of those most closely involved in coördinating the effort, lapsed; provincial factions were reverting to the old provincial ways. The impulse to arrest disorder and to revive the flame of revolutionary unity may be pictured in "conservative" terms, but this becomes quite awkward when we look for terms with which to picture the other impulse, so different in nature: the urge to rest, to drift, to turn back the clock.

Various writers have said that the activities of the Federalists during this period had in them a clear element of the conspiratorial. Insofar as this refers to a strong line of political strategy, it correctly locates a key element in the movement. Yet without a growing base of popular dissatisfaction with the status quo, the Federalists could have skulked and plotted forever without accomplishing anything. We now know, thanks to recent scholarship, that numerous elements of the public were only too ripe for change. But the work of organizing such a sentiment was quite another matter; it took an immense effort of will just to get it off the ground. Though it would be wrong to think of the Constitution as something that had to be carried in the face of deep and basic popular opposition, it certainly required a series of brilliant maneuvers to escape the deadening clutch of particularism and inertia. An Anti-Federalist "no" could register on exactly the same plane as a Federalist "yes" while requiring a fraction of the energy. It was for this reason that the Federalists, even though they cannot be said to have circumvented the popular will, did have to use techniques which in their sustained drive, tactical mobility, and risk-taking smacked more than a little of the revolutionary.

By 1781, nearly five years of intimate experience with the war effort had already convinced such men as Washington, Madison, Hamilton, Duane, and Wilson that something had to be done to strengthen the Continental government, at least to the point of providing it with an independent income. The ratification of the Articles of Confederation early in the year (before Yorktown) seemed to offer a new chance, and several promising steps were taken at that time. Congress organized executive departments of war, foreign affairs, and finance to replace unwieldy and inefficient committees; Robert Morris was appointed Superintendent of Finance; and a 5 per cent impost was passed which Congress urged the states to accept.

By the fall of 1782, however, the surge for increased efficiency had lost the greater part of its momentum. Virginia had changed its mind about accepting the impost, Rhode Island having been flatly opposed all along, and it became apparent that as soon as the treaty with England (then being completed) was ratified, the sense of common purpose which the war had created would be drained of its urgency. At this point Hamilton and the Morrises, desperate for a solution, would have been quite willing to use the discontent of an unpaid army as a threat to coerce the states out of their obstructionism, had not Washington refused to lend himself to any such scheme. Madison and Hamilton thereupon joined forces in Congress to work out a revenue bill whose subsidiary benefits would be sufficiently diffuse to gain it general support among the states. But

in the end the best that could be managed was a new plan for a 5 per cent impost, the revenues of which would be collected by state-appointed officials. Once more an appeal, drafted by Madison, was sent to the states urging them to accept the new impost, and Washington wrote a circular in support of it. The effort was in vain. The army, given one month's pay in cash and three in certificates, reluctantly dispersed, and the Confederation government, with no sanctions of coercion and no assured revenues, now reached a new level of impotence. In June, 1783, Alexander Hamilton, preparing to leave Congress to go back to private life, wrote in discouragement and humiliation to Nathanael Greene:

> There is so little disposition either in or out of Congress to give solidity to our national system that there is no motive to a man to lose his time in the public service, who has no other view than to promote its welfare. Experience must convince us that our present establishments are Utopian before we shall be ready to part with them for better.

Whether or not the years between 1783 and 1786 should be viewed as a "critical period" depends very much on whose angle they are viewed from. Although it was a time of economic depression, the depressed conditions were not felt in all areas of economic life with the same force, nor were they nearly as damaging in some localities as in others; the interdependence of economic enterprise was not then what it would become later on, and a depression in Massachusetts did not necessarily imply one in Virginia, or even in New York. Moreover, there were definite signs of improvement by 1786. Nor can it necessarily be said that government on the state level lacked vitality. Most of the states were addressing their problems with energy and decision. There were problems everywhere, of course, many of them very grave, and in some cases (those of New Jersey and Connecticut in particular) solutions seemed almost beyond the individual state's resources. Yet it would be wrong, as Merrill Jensen points out, to assume that no solutions were possible within the framework which then existed. It is especially important to remember that when most people thought of "the government" they were not thinking of Congress at all, but of their own state legislature. For them, therefore, it was by no means self-evident that the period through which they were living was one of drift and governmental impotence.

But through the eyes of men who had come to view the states collectively as a "country" and to think in continental terms, things looked altogether different. From their viewpoint the Confederation was fast approaching the point of ruin. Fewer and fewer states were meeting their requisition payments, and Congress could not even pay its bills. The states refused to accept any impost which they themselves could not control, and even if all the rest accepted, the continued refusal of New York (which was not likely to change) would render any impost all but valueless. Local fears and jealousies blocked all efforts to establish uniform regulation of commerce, even though some such regulation seemed indispensable. A number of the states, New York in particular, openly ignored the peace treaty with England and passed discriminatory legislation against former Loyalists; consequently England, using as a pretext Congress' inability to enforce the treaty, refused to surrender the northwest posts. Morale in Congress was very low as members complained that lack of a quorum prevented them most of the

time from transacting any business; even when a quorum was present, a few negative votes could block important legislation indefinitely. Any significant change, or any substantial increase in the power of Congress, required unanimous approval by the states, and as things then stood this had become very remote. Finally, major states such as New York and Virginia were simply paying less and less attention to Congress. The danger was not so much that of a split with the Confederation—Congress lacked the strength that would make any such "split" seem very urgent—but rather a policy of neglect that would just allow Congress to wither away from inactivity.

These were the conditions that set the stage for a fresh effort—the Annapolis Convention of 1786—to strengthen the continental government. The year before, Madison had arranged a conference between Maryland and Virginia for the regulation of commerce on the Potomac, and its success had led John Tyler and Madison to propose a measure in the Virginia Assembly that would give Congress power to regulate commerce throughout the Confederation. Though nothing came of it, a plan was devised in its place whereby the several states would be invited to take part in a convention to be held at Annapolis in September, 1786, for the purpose of discussing commercial problems. The snapping-point came when delegates from only five states appeared. The rest either distrusted one another's intentions (the northeastern states doubted the southerners' interest in commerce) or else suspected a trick to strengthen the Confederation government at their expense. It was apparent that no serious action could be taken at that time. But the dozen delegates who did come (Hamilton and Madison being in their forefront) were by definition those most concerned over the state of the national government, and they soon concluded that their only hope of saving it lay in some audacious plenary gesture. It was at this meeting, amid the mortification of still another failure, that they planned the Philadelphia Convention.

The revolutionary character of this move—though some writers have correctly perceived it—has been obscured both by the stateliness of historical retrospection and by certain legal peculiarities which allowed the proceeding to appear a good deal less subversive than it actually was. The "report" of the Annapolis meeting was actually a call, drafted by Hamilton and carefully edited by Madison, for delegates of all the states to meet in convention at Philadelphia the following May for the purpose of revising the Articles of Confederation. Congress itself transmitted the call, and in so doing was in effect being brought to by-pass its own constituted limits. On the one hand, any effort to change the government within the rules laid down by the Articles would have required a unanimous approval which could never be obtained. But on the other hand, the very helplessness which the several states had imposed upon the central government meant in practice that the states were sovereign and could do anything they pleased with it. It was precisely this that the nationalists now prepared to exploit: this legal paradox had hitherto prevented the growth of strong loyalty to the existing Confederation and could presently allow that same Confederation, through the action of the states, to be undermined in the deceptive odor of legitimacy. Thus the Beardian school of constitutional thought, for all its errors of economic analysis and its transposing of ideological

semantics, has called attention to one element—the element of subversion—that is actually entitled to some consideration.

But if the movement had its plotters, balance requires us to add that the "plot" now had a considerable measure of potential support, and that the authority against which the plot was aimed had become little more than a husk. Up to this time every nationalist move, including the Annapolis Convention, had been easily blocked. But things were now happening in such a way as to tip the balance and to offer the nationalists for the first time a better-than-even chance of success. There had been a marked improvement in business, but shippers in Boston, New York, and Philadelphia were still in serious trouble. Retaliatory measures against Great Britain through state legislation had proved ineffective and useless; there was danger, at the same time, that local manufacturing interests might be successful in pushing through high state tariffs. In the second place, New York's refusal to reconsider a national impost, except on terms that would have removed its effectiveness, cut the ground from under the moderates who had argued that, given only a little time, everything could be worked out. This did not leave much alternative to a major revision of the national government. Then there were Rhode Island's difficulties with inflationary paper money. Although that state's financial schemes actually made a certain amount of sense, they provided the nationalists with wonderful propaganda and helped to create an image of parochial irresponsibility.

The most decisive event of all was Shays' Rebellion in the fall and winter of 1786–1787. It was this uprising of hard-pressed rural debtors in western Massachusetts that frightened moderate people everywhere and convinced them of the need for drastic remedies against what looked like anarchy. The important thing was not so much the facts of the case as the impression which it created outside Massachusetts. The Shaysites had no intention of destroying legitimate government or of redistributing property, but the fact that large numbers of people could very well imagine them doing such things added a note of crisis which was all to the Federalists' advantage. Even the level-headed Washington was disturbed, and his apprehensions were played upon quite knowingly by Madison, Hamilton, and Knox in persuading him to attend the Philadelphia Convention. Actually the Federalists and the Shaysites had been driven to action by much the same conditions; in Massachusetts their concern with the depressed state of trade and the tax burden placed them for all practical purposes on the same side, and there they remained from first to last.

Once the balance had been tipped in enough states, to the point of a working consensus on the desirability of change, a second principle came into effect. Unless a state were absolutely opposed—as in the extreme case of Rhode Island—to any change in the Articles of Confederation, it was difficult to ignore the approaching Philadelphia Convention as had been done with the Annapolis Convention: the occasion was taking on too much importance. There was thus the danger, for such a state, of seeing significant decisions made without having its interests consulted. New York, with strong Anti-Federalist biases but also with a strong nationalist undercurrent, was not quite willing to boycott the convention. Governor Clinton's solution was to send as delegates two rigid state particularists,

John Yates and Robert Lansing, along with the nationalist Hamilton, to make sure that Hamilton would not accomplish anything.

We have already seen that nineteenth century habits of thought created a ponderous array of stereotypes around the historic Philadelphia conclave of 1787. Twentieth century thought and scholarship, on the other hand, had the task of breaking free from them, and to have done so is a noteworthy achievement. And yet one must return to the point that stereotypes themselves require some form of explanation. The legend of a transcendent effort of statesmanship, issuing forth in a miraculously perfect instrument of government, emerges again and again despite all efforts either to conjure it out of existence or to give it some sort of rational linkage with mortal affairs. Why should the legend be so extraordinarily durable, and was there anything so special about the circumstances that set it on its way so unerringly and so soon?

The circumstances *were*, in fact, special; given a set of delegates of well over average ability, the Philadelphia meeting provides a really classic study in the sociology of intellect. Divine accident, though in some measure present in men's doings always, is not required as a part of this particular equation. The key conditions were all present in a pattern that virtually guaranteed for the meeting an optimum of effectiveness. A sufficient number of states were represented so that the delegates could, without strain, realistically picture themselves as thinking, acting, and making decisions in the name of the entire nation. They themselves, moreover, represented interests throughout the country that were diverse enough, and they had enough personal prestige at home, that they could act in the assurance of having their decisions treated at least with respectful attention. There had also been at work a remarkably effective process of self-selection, as to both men and states. Rhode Island ignored the convention, and as a result its position was not even considered there. There were leading state particularists such as Patrick Henry and Richard Henry Lee who were elected as delegates but refused to serve. The Anti-Federalist position, indeed, was hardly represented at all, and the few men who did represent it had surprisingly little to say. Yates and Lansing simply left before the convention was over. Thus a group already predisposed in a national direction could proceed unhampered by the friction of basic opposition in its midst.

This made it possible for the delegates to "try on" various alternatives without having to remain accountable for everything they said. At the same time, being relieved from all outside pressures meant that the only way a man could expect to make a real difference in the convention's deliberations was to reach, through main persuasion, other men of considerable ability and experience. Participants and audience were therefore one, and this in itself imposed standards of debate which were quite exacting. In such a setting the best minds in the convention were accorded an authority which they would not have had in political debates aimed at an indiscriminate public.

Thus the elements of secrecy, the general inclination for a national government, and the process whereby the delegates came to terms with their colleagues —appreciating their requirements and adjusting to their interests—all combined to produce a growing esprit de corps. As initial agreements were worked out, it became exceedingly difficult for the Philadelphia delegates not to grow more and more committed to the product of their joint efforts. Indeed, this was in all likelihood the key mechanism, more important than any other in explaining not only the peculiar genius of the main compromises but also the general fitness of the document as a whole. That is, a group of two or more intelligent men who are subject to no cross-pressures and whose principal commitment is to the success of an idea, are perfectly capable—as in our scientific communities of today—of performing what appear to be prodigies of intellect. Moving, as it were, in the same direction with a specific purpose, they can function at maximum efficiency. It was this that the historians of the nineteenth century did in their way see, and celebrated with sweeping rhetorical flourishes, when they took for granted that if an occasion of this sort could not call forth the highest level of statesmanship available, then it was impossible to imagine another that could.

Once the Philadelphia Convention had been allowed to meet and the delegates had managed, after more than three months of work, to hammer out a document that the great majority of them could sign, the political position of the Federalists changed dramatically. Despite the major battles still impending, for practical purposes they now had the initiative. The principal weapon of the Anti-Federalists—inertia—had greatly declined in effectiveness, for with the new program in motion it was no longer enough simply to argue that a new federal government was unnecessary. They would have to take positive steps in blocking it; they would have to arouse the people and convince them that the Constitution represented a positive danger.

Moreover, the Federalists had set the terms of ratification in such a way as to give the maximum advantage to energy and purpose; the key choices, this time, had been so arranged that they would fall right. Only nine states had to ratify before the Constitution would go into effect. Not only would this rule out the possibility of one or two states holding up the entire effort, but it meant that the Confederation would be automatically destroyed as an alternative before the difficult battles in New York and Virginia had to be faced. (By then, Patrick Henry in Virginia would have nothing but a vague alliance with North Carolina to offer as a counter-choice.) Besides, there was good reason to believe that at least four or five states, and possibly as many as seven, could be counted as safe, which meant that serious fighting in the first phase would be limited to two or three states. And finally, conditions were so set that the "snowball" principle would at each successive point favor the Federalists.

As for the actual process of acceptance, ratification would be done through state conventions elected for the purpose. Not only would this circumvent the vested interests of the legislatures and the ruling coteries that frequented the state capitals, but it gave the Federalists two separate chances to make their case—once to the people and once to the conventions. If the elected delegates were not initially disposed to do the desired thing, there was still a chance, after the convention met, of persuading them. Due partly to the hampering factor of transportation and distance, delegates had to have considerable leeway of choice and what amounted to quasi-plenipotentiary powers. Thus there could be no such thing as a fully "instructed" delegation, and members might meanwhile remain susceptible to argument and conversion. The convention device, moreover, enabled the Federalists to run as delegates

men who would not normally take part in state politics.

The revolutionary verve and ardor of the Federalists, their resources of will and energy, their willingness to scheme tirelessly, campaign everywhere, and sweat and agonize over every vote meant in effect that despite all the hairbreadth squeezes and rigors of the struggle, the Anti-Federalists would lose every crucial test. There was, to be sure, an Anti-Federalist effort. But with no program, no really viable commitments, and little purposeful organization, the Anti-Federalists somehow always managed to move too late and with too little. They would sit and watch their great stronghold, New York, being snatched away from them despite a two-to-one Anti-Federalists majority in a convention presided over by their own chief, George Clinton. To them, the New York Federalists must have seemed possessed of the devil. The Federalists' convention men included Alexander Hamilton, James Duane, John Jay, and Robert Livingston —who knew, as did everyone else, that the new government was doomed unless Virginia and New York joined it. They insisted on debating the Constitution section by section instead of as a whole, which meant that they could out-argue the Anti-Federalists on every substantive issue and meanwhile delay the vote until New Hampshire and Virginia had had a chance to ratify. (Madison and Hamilton had a horse relay system in readiness to rush the Virginia news northward as quickly as possible.) By the time the New York convention was ready to act, ten others had ratified, and at the final moment Hamilton and his allies spread the chilling rumor that New York City was about to secede from the state. The Anti-Federalists, who had had enough, directed a chosen number of their delegates to cross over, and solemnly capitulated.

In the end, of course, everyone "crossed over." The speed with which this occurred once the continental revolutionists had made their point, and the ease with which the Constitution so soon became an object of universal veneration, still stands as one of the minor marvels of American history. But the document did contain certain implications, of a quasi-philosophical nature, that make the reasons for this ready consensus not so very difficult to find. It established a national government whose basic outlines were sufficiently congenial to the underlying commitments of the whole culture—republicanism and capitalism—that the likelihood of its being the subject of a true ideological clash was never very real. That the Constitution should mount guard over the rights of property—"realty," "personalty," or any other kind—was questioned by nobody. There had certainly been a struggle, a long and exhausting one, but we should not be deceived as to its nature. It was not fought on economic grounds; it was not a matter of ideology; it was not, in the fullest and most fundamental sense, even a struggle between nationalism and localism. The key struggle was between inertia and energy; with inertia overcome, everything changed.

There were, of course, lingering objections and misgivings; many of the problems involved had been genuinely puzzling and difficult; and there remained doubters who had to be converted. But then the perfect bridge whereby all could become Federalists within a year was the addition of a Bill of Rights. After the French Revolution, anti-constitutionalism in France would be a burning issue for generations; in America, an anti-constitutional party was undreamed of after 1789. With the Bill of Rights, the remaining opponents of the new system could say that, ever watchful of tyranny, they had now got what they wanted. Moreover, the Young Men of the Revolution might at last imagine, after a dozen years of anxiety, that *their* Revolution had been a success.

MARTIN DIAMOND (1919–   ) is in the Political
Science Department at Claremont Men's College,
California. In this selection, Mr. Diamond shows what
he considers to be the essential agreement of the
Declaration of Independence and the Constitution.
By so doing, he frees the Declaration from the charge
of ignoring the problems of popular government and
puts some of the motivation for the Constitution to the
necessity of realizing the promise of the Declaration.
The author believes this promise, the formation of
a popular government, was realized in the Constitution,
and in a way which guarded against the abuses of
democracy without compromising any of its principles.
His affirmation of the democratic character of the
Constitution runs directly counter to Charles Beard's
view of it as a document designed to protect property
and preserve aristocratic rule.*

Martin Diamond

A Democratic Cure for the
"Diseases" and "Defects" of Democracy

Our major political problems today are
problems of democracy; and, as much as
anything else, the *Federalist* papers are a
teaching about democracy. The conclusion of one of the most important of these
papers states what is also the most important theme in the entire work: the
necessity for "a republican remedy for
the diseases most incident to republican
government." The theme is clearly repeated in a passage where Thomas Jefferson is praised for displaying equally
"a fervent attachment to republican government and an enlightened view of the
dangerous propensities against which it
ought to be guarded." *The Federalist*,
thus, stresses its commitment to republi-

can or popular government, but, of
course, insists that this must be an enlightened commitment.

But *The Federalist* and the Founding
Fathers generally have not been taken
at their word. Predominantly, they are
understood as being only quasi- or even
anti-democrats. Modern American historical writing, at least until very recently, has generally seen the Constitution as some sort of apostasy from, or
reaction to, the radically democratic
implications of the Declaration of Independence—a reaction that was undone by
the great "democratic breakthroughs" of
Jeffersonianism, Jacksonianism, etc. This
view, I believe, involves a false under-

*Reprinted by permission from Martin Diamond, "Democracy and *The Federalist:* A Reconsideration
of the Framers' Intents," *American Political Science Review*, LIII, No. 1 (March, 1959), 53–61. Footnotes
omitted.

standing of the crucial political issues involved in the founding of the American Republic. Further, it is based implicitly upon a questionable modern approach to democracy and has tended to have the effect, moreover, of relegating the political teaching of the Founding Fathers to the pre-democratic past and thus of making it of no vital concern to moderns. The Founding Fathers themselves repeatedly stressed that their Constitution was wholly consistent with the true principles of republican or popular government. The prevailing modern opinion, in varying degrees and in different ways, rejects that claim. It thus becomes important to understand what was the relation of the Founding Fathers to popular government or democracy.

I have deliberately used interchangeably their terms, "popular government" and "democracy." The Founding Fathers, of course, did not use the terms entirely synonymously and the idea that they were less than "democrats" has been fortified by the fact that they sometimes defined "democracy" invidiously in comparison with "republic." But this fact does not really justify the opinion. For their basic view was that *popular government was the genus, and democracy and republic were two species* of that genus of government. What distinguished popular government from other genera of government was that in it, political authority is "derived from the great body of the society, not from . . . [any] favoured class of it." With respect to this decisive question, of where political authority is lodged, democracy and republic—as *The Federalist* uses the terms—differ not in the least. Republics, equally with democracies, may claim to be wholly a form of popular government. This is neither to deny the difference between the two, nor to depreciate the importance *The Fed-*

eralist attached to the difference; but in *The Federalist's* view, the difference does not relate to the essential principle of popular government. Democracy means in *The Federalist* that form of popular government where the citizens "assemble and administer the government in person." Republics differ in that the people rule through representatives and, of course, in the consequences of that difference. The crucial point is that republics and democracies are equally forms of popular government, but that the one form is vastly preferable to the other because of the substantive consequences of the difference in form. Those historians who consider the Founding Fathers as less than "democrats," miss or reject the Founders' central contention that, while being perfectly faithful to the *principle* of popular government, they had solved the *problem* of popular government.

In what way is the Constitution ordinarily thought to be less democratic than the Declaration? The argument is usually that the former is characterized by fear of the people, by preoccupation with minority interests and rights, and by measures therefore taken against the power of majorities. The Declaration, it is true, does not display these features, but this is no proof of a fundamental difference of principle between the two. Is it not obviously possible that the difference is due only to a difference in the tasks to which the two documents were addressed? And is it not further possible that the democratic principles of the Declaration are not only compatible with the prophylactic measures of the Constitution, but actually imply them?

The Declaration of Independence formulates two criteria for judging whether any government is good, or indeed legitimate. Good government must rest, procedurally, upon the consent of the governed. Good government, substantively, must do only certain things, *e.g.*, secure certain rights. This may be stated another way by borrowing a phrase from Locke, appropriate enough when discussing the Declaration. That "the people shall be judge" is of the essence of democracy, is its peculiar form or method of proceeding. That the people shall judge rightly is the substantive problem of democracy. But whether the procedure will bring about the substance is problematic. Between the Declaration's two criteria, then, a tension exists: consent can be given or obtained for governmental actions which are not right—at least as the men of 1776 saw the right. (To give an obvious example from their point of view: the people may freely but wrongly vote away the protection due to property.) Thus the Declaration clearly contained, although it did not resolve, a fundamental problem. Solving the problem was not its task; that was the task for the framers of the Constitution. But the man who wrote the Declaration of Independence and the leading men who supported it were perfectly aware of the difficulty, and of the necessity for a "republican remedy."

What the text of the Declaration, taken alone, tells of its meaning may easily be substantiated by the testimony of its author and supporters. Consider only that Jefferson, with no known change of heart at all, said of *The Federalist* that it was "the best commentary on the principles of government which was ever written." Jefferson, it must be remembered, came firmly to recommend the adoption of the Constitution, his criticisms of it having come down only to a proposal for rotation in the Presidency and for the subsequent adoption of a bill of rights. I do not, of course, deny the

peculiar character of "Jeffersonianism" nor the importance to many things of its proper understanding. I only state here that it is certain that Jefferson, unlike later historians, did not view the Constitution as a retrogression from democracy. Or further, consider that John Adams, now celebrated as America's great conservative, was so enthusiastic about Jefferson's draft of the Declaration as to wish on his own account that hardly a word be changed. And this same Adams, also without any change of heart and without complaint, accepted the Constitution as embodying many of his own views on government.

The idea that the Constitution was a falling back from the fuller democracy of the Declaration thus rests in part upon a false reading of the Declaration as free from the concerns regarding democracy that the framers of the Constitution felt. Perhaps only those would so read it who take for granted a perfect, self-subsisting harmony between consent (equality) and the proper aim of government (justice), or between consent and individual rights (liberty). This assumption was utterly foreign to the leading men of the Declaration.

The Declaration has wrongly been converted into, as it were, a super-democratic document; has the Constitution wrongly been converted in the modern view into an insufficiently democratic document? The only basis for depreciating the democratic character of the Constitution lies in its framers' apprehensive diagnosis of the "diseases," "defects" or "evil propensities" of democracy, and in their remedies. But if what the Founders considered to be defects *are* genuine defects, and if the remedies, without violating the principles of popular government, *are* genuine remedies, then it would be unreasonable to call the Founders anti- or quasi-democrats. Rather, they would be the wise partisans of democracy; a man is not a better democrat but only a foolish democrat if he ignores real defects inherent in popular government. Thus, the question becomes: are there natural defects to democracy and, if there are, what are the best remedies?

In part, the Founding Fathers answered this question by employing a traditional mode of political analysis. They believed there were several basic possible regimes, each having several possible forms. Of these possible regimes they believed the best, or at least the best for America, to be popular government, but only if purged of its defects. At any rate, an unpurged popular government they believed to be indefensible. They believed there were several forms of popular government, crucial among these direct democracy and republican—or representative—government (the latter perhaps divisible into two distinct forms, large and small republics). Their constitution and their defense of it constitute an argument for that form of popular government (large republic) in which the "evil propensities" would be weakest or most susceptible of remedy.

The whole of the thought of the Founding Fathers is intelligible and, especially, the evaluation of their claim to be wise partisans of popular government is possible, only if the words *"disease," "defect,"* and *"evil propensity"* are allowed their full force. Unlike modern "value-free" social scientists, the Founding Fathers believed that true knowledge of the good and bad in human conduct was possible, and that they themselves possessed sufficient knowledge to discern the really grave defects of popular government and their proper remedies. The modern relativistic or positivistic theories, implicitly employed by most commentators on the Founding Fathers, deny the possibility of such true knowledge and therefore deny that the Founding Fathers *could* have been actuated by knowledge of the good rather than by passion or interest. (I deliberately employ the language of *Federalist* No. 10. Madison defined faction, in part, as a group "united and actuated by . . . passion, or . . . interest." That is, factions are groups *not*—as presumably the authors of *The Federalist* were—actuated by reason.) How this modern view of the value problem supports the conception of the Constitution as less democratic than the Declaration is clear. The Founding Fathers did in fact seek to prejudice the outcome of democracy; they sought to alter, by certain restraints, the likelihood that the majority would decide certain political issues in bad ways. These restraints the Founders justified as mitigating the natural defects of democracy. But, say the moderns, there are no "bad" political decisions, wrong-in-themselves, from reaching which the majority ought to be restrained. Therefore, ultimately, nothing other than the specific interests of the Founders can explain their zeal in restraining democracy. And inasmuch as the restraints were typically placed on the many in the interest of the propertied, the departure of the Constitution is "anti-democratic" or "thermidorean." In short, according to this view, there cannot be what the Founders claimed to possess, "an *enlightened* view of the dangerous propensities against which [popular government] . . . ought to be guarded," the substantive goodness or badness of such propensities being a matter of opinion or taste on which reason can shed no light.

What are some of the arrangements which have been considered signs of "undemocratic" features of the Constitution? The process by which the Constitution may be amended is often cited in evidence. Everyone is familiar with the arithmetic which shows that a remarkably small minority could prevent passage of a constitutional amendment supported by an overwhelming majority of the people. That is, bare majorities in the thirteen least populous states could prevent passage of an amendment desired by overwhelming majorities in the thirty-six most populous states. But let us, for a reason to be made clear in a moment, turn that arithmetic around. Bare majorities in the thirty-seven least populous states can pass amendments against the opposition of overwhelming majorities in the twelve most populous states. And this would mean in actual votes today (and would have meant for the thirteen original states) constitutional amendment by a minority against the opposition of a majority of citizens. My point is simply that, while the amending procedure does involve qualified majorities, the qualification is not of the kind that requires an especially large numerical majority for action.

I suggest that the real aim and practical effect of the complicated amending procedure was not at all to give power to minorities, but to ensure that passage of an amendment would require a *nationally* distributed majority, though one that legally could consist of a bare numerical majority. It was only adventitious that the procedure has the theoretical possibility of a minority blocking (or passing) an amendment. The aim of requiring nationally distributed majorities was, I think, to ensure that no amendment could be passed simply with the support of the few states or sections sufficiently numerous to provide a bare majority. No doubt it was also believed that it would

be difficult for such a national majority to form or become effective save for the decent purposes that could command national agreement, and this difficulty was surely deemed a great virtue of the amending process. This is what I think *The Federalist* really means when it praises the amending process and says that "it guards equally against that extreme facility, which would render the Constitution too mutable; and that extreme difficulty, which might perpetuate its discovered faults." All I wish to emphasize here is that the actual method adopted, with respect to the numerical size of majorities, is meant to leave all legal power in the hands of ordinary majorities so long as they are national majorities. The departure from simple majoritarianism is, at least, not in an oligarchic or aristocratic direction. In this crucial respect, the amending procedure does conform strictly to the principles of republican (popular) government.

Consider next the suffrage question. It has long been assumed as proof of an anti-democratic element in the Constitution that the Founding Fathers depended for the working of their Constitution upon a substantially limited franchise. Just as the Constitution allegedly was ratified by a highly qualified electorate, so too, it is held, was the new government to be based upon a suffrage subject to substantial property qualifications. This view has only recently been seriously challenged, especially by Robert E. Brown, whose detailed researches convince him that the property qualifications in nearly all the original states were probably so small as to exclude never more than twenty-five per cent, and in most cases as little as only five to ten per cent, of the adult white male population. That is, the property qualifications were not designed to exclude the mass of the poor but only the small proportion which lacked a concrete—however small—stake in society, *i.e.*, primarily the transients or "idlers."

The Constitution, of course, left the suffrage question to the decision of the individual states. What is the implication of that fact for deciding what sort of suffrage the Framers had in mind? The immediately popular branch of the national legislature was to be elected by voters who "shall have the qualifications requisite for electors of the most numerous branch of the State Legislature." The mode of election to the electoral college for the Presidency and to the Senate is also left to "be prescribed in each State by the legislature thereof." At a minimum, it may be stated that the Framers did not themselves attempt to reduce, or prevent the expansion of, the suffrage; that question was left wholly to the states —and these were, ironically, the very hotbeds of post-revolutionary democracy from the rule of which it is familiarly alleged that the Founders sought to escape.

In general, the conclusion seems inescapable that the states had a far broader suffrage than is ordinarily thought, and nothing in the actions of the Framers suggests any expectation or prospect of the reduction of the suffrage. Again, as in the question of the amending process, I suggest that the Constitution represented no departure whatsoever from the democratic standards of the Revolutionary period, or from any democratic standards then generally recognized.

What of the Senate? The organization of the Senate, its term of office and its staggered mode of replacement, its election by state legislatures rather than directly by the people, among other things, have been used to demonstrate the un-democratic character of the Senate as intended by the Framers. Was this not a device to represent property and not people, and was it not intended therefore to be a non-popular element in the government? I suggest, on the contrary, that the really important thing is that the Framers thought they had found a way to protect property *without* representing it. That the Founders intended the Senate to be one of the crucial devices for remedying the defects of democracy is certainly true. But *The Federalist* argues that the Senate, as actually proposed in the Constitution, was calculated to be such a device as would operate only in a way that "will consist . . . with the genuine principles of republican government." I believe that the claim is just.

Rather than viewing the Senate from the perspective of modern experience and opinions, consider how radically democratic the Senate appears when viewed from a pre-modern perspective. The model of a divided legislature that the Founders had most in mind was probably the English Parliament. There the House of Lords was thought to provide some of the beneficial checks upon the popular Commons which it was hoped the Senate would supply in the American Constitution. But the American Senate was to possess none of the qualities which permitted the House of Lords to fulfill its role; *i.e.*, its hereditary basis, or membership upon election by the Crown, or any of its other aristocratic characteristics. Yet the Founding Fathers knew that the advantages of having both a Senate and a House would "be in proportion to the dissimilarity in the genius of the two bodies." What is remarkable is that, in seeking to secure this dissimilarity, they did not in any respect go beyond the limits permitted by the "genuine principles of republican government."

Not only is this dramatically demonstrated in comparison with the English House of Lords, but also in comparison with all earlier theory regarding the division of the legislative power. The aim of such a division in earlier thought is to secure a balance between the aristocratic and democratic elements of a polity. This is connected with the pre-modern preference for a *mixed* republic, which was rejected by the Founders in favor of a *democratic* republic. And the traditional way to secure this balance or mixture was to give one house or office to the suffrages of the few and one to the suffrages of the many. Nothing of the kind is involved in the American Senate. Indeed, on this issue, so often cited as evidence of the Founders' undemocratic predilections, the very opposite is the case. The Senate is a constitutional device which *par excellence* reveals the strategy of the Founders. They wanted something like the advantages earlier thinkers had seen in a mixed legislative power, but they thought this was possible (and perhaps preferable) without any introduction whatsoever of aristocratic power into their system. What premodern thought had seen in an aristocratic senate—wisdom, nobility, manners, religion, etc.—the Founding Fathers converted into stability, enlightened self-interest, a "temperate and respectable body of citizens." The qualities of a senate having thus been altered (involving perhaps comparable changes in the notion of the ends of government), it became possible to secure these advantages through a Senate based wholly upon popular principles. Or so I would characterize a Senate whose membership required no property qualification and which was appointed (or elected in the manner prescribed) by State legislatures which, in their own turn, were elected annually or biennially by a nearly universal manhood suffrage.

The great claim of *The Federalist* is that the Constitution represents the fulfillment of a truly novel experiment, of "a revolution which has no parallel in the annals of society," and which is decisive for the happiness of "the whole human race." And the novelty, I argue, consisted in solving the problems of popular government by means which yet maintain the government "wholly popular." In defending that claim against the idea of the Constitution as a retreat from democracy I have dealt thus far only with the easier task: the demonstration that the constitutional devices and arrangements do not derogate from the legal power of majorities to rule. What remains is to examine the claim that the Constitution did in fact remedy the natural defects of democracy. Before any effort is made in this direction, it may be useful to summarize some of the implications and possible utility of the analysis thus far.

Above all, the merit of the suggestions I have made, if they are accurate in describing the intention and action of the Founders, is that it makes the Founders available to us for the study of modern problems. I have tried to restore to them their *bona fides* as partisans of democracy. This done, we may take seriously the question whether they were, as they claimed to be, wise partisans of democracy or popular government. If they were partisans of democracy and if the regime they created was decisively democratic, then they speak to us not merely about bygone problems, not from a viewpoint—in this regard—radically different from our own, but as men addressing themselves to problems identical in principle with our own. They are a source from within our own heritage which teaches us the way to put the question to democracy, a way which is rejected by certain prevailing modern ideas. But we cannot avail ourselves of their assistance if we consider American history to be a succession of democratizations which overcame the Founding Fathers' intentions. On that view it is easy to regard them as simply outmoded. If I am right regarding the extent of democracy in their thought and regime, then they are not outmoded by modern events but rather are tested by them. American history, on this view, is not primarily the replacement of a pre-democratic regime by a democratic regime, but is rather a continuing testimony to how the Founding Fathers' democratic regime has worked out in modern circumstances. The whole of our national experience thus becomes a way of judging the Founders' principles, of judging democracy itself, or of pondering the flaws of democracy and the means to its improvement.

ROBERT E. BROWN (1907–   ) is Professor of
American History at Michigan State University. His
Charles A. Beard and the Constitution was written after
he became convinced that Beard's view of the formation
of the Constitution was almost entirely incorrect. In
Brown's view, the Constitution did safeguard property
but this served the interests of the majority of
Americans who were middle-class freeholders. These
freeholders possessed the right to vote and used it when
they saw significant issues in electoral contests. If they
did not vote in the ratification contests, it was because
they could see no ill effects coming from the
Constitution.*

Robert E. Brown

A Government by and for the Majority

Having reviewed all this evidence on the economic holdings of the Convention delegates, the important question is whether Beard's historical method justified his conclusions that personal property was responsible for the Constitution. The answer must be an emphatic no. If we forget Beard's own generalizations and consider only his evidence, we find that actually only six delegates had personal property in excess of their realty (Clymer, Fitzsimons, Gilman, Gerry, Robert Morris, and Williamson), and further research into their holdings might show that even some of these held more realty than personalty. Two of these are of questionable value as evidence, Gilman because he presumably wanted

farmers as well as personalty interests to benefit, and Gerry because he opposed the Constitution in spite of his holdings. In contrast with these six, and again strictly on the basis of Beard's evidence, eighteen delegates definitely had realty which greatly outweighed their personalty (Bassett, Bedford, Blount, Carroll, Davie, Dickinson, Few, Jenifer, Madison, Alexander Martin, Mason, Gouverneur Morris, Charles Cotesworth Pinckney, Charles Pinckney, Rutledge, Spaight, Washington, and Wythe). The other thirty (Baldwin, Blair, Brearley, Broom, Butler, Dayton, Ellsworth, Franklin, Gorham, Hamilton, Houston, Houstoun, Ingersoll, Johnson, King, Langdon, Lansing, Livingston, Luther Martin,

*Reprinted from Robert E. Brown, *Charles A. Beard and the Constitution: A Critical Analysis of "An Economic Interpretation of the Constitution"* (Princeton, N.J.; copyright © 1956 by Princeton University Press), pp. 89–94, 97–101, 105–111, 142–148, 157–158, 159–160, 164–165, 196–200. Reprinted by permission of Princeton University Press. Footnotes omitted.

84

McClurg, McHenry, Mercer, Mifflin, Paterson, Pierce, Randolph, Read, Sherman, Strong, and Wilson) really prove nothing in particular on the basis of Beard's evidence, for even he could not tell what these men had in the way of economic goods. . . .

Anyone would concede that the Founding Fathers had education, property, and influence far greater than the average at that time, but the same would be true of colonial legislatures, the Confederation Congress, and legislatures today. Had Beard cited this evidence to prove that the Convention delegates represented property in general and were interested in a government which would protect property, he would have been on firm ground. All of the delegates believed in the sanctity of property; some even believed that the chief function of government was the protection of property. This was undoubtedly important, but it was not their only concern. Beard did not contend, however, that the Convention was rigged to protect property *in general.* What he emphasized was *personalty,* and in fact, a particular kind of personalty which did not include livestock and slaves. We shall see later that he even refined personal property to mean predominantly one kind of personal property—public securities.

In addition to the fact that the evidence in this chapter does not prove the predominance of personalty, the big criticism of this particular economic interpretation is the ease with which Beard dismissed the agricultural interest. Does this mean that farmers had no economic interests? Would a politician in the predominantly agricultural states of North and South Dakota ignore the farm vote in his state? Yet in 1787 all the states were more agricultural than the Dakotas.

As Shays' Rebellion and Washington's inability to pay his taxes demonstrated, the farmers as well as the holders of personalty were not enjoying prosperous times. Why not assume that perhaps they, too, expected conditions to be better under the new government? And why draw such a sharp distinction between realty and various forms of personalty? A man who owns realty is not necessarily less interested in his property than anyone else. The simple fact is that the farmers cannot be ignored in the adoption of the Constitution, for as we shall see, some of the most heavily agricultural states adopted the Constitution the most quickly and by the most nearly unanimous vote. He who leaves the farmers out of the picture of the Constitution is treading on thin ice indeed, especially when such an important man as Washington was so obviously on the side of realty.

Having proved to his own satisfaction that the delegates to the Convention were the representatives of personalty, Beard then went on to show that the Constitution was fundamentally an economic rather than a political document, designed above all else to protect personalty from the leveling attacks of democracy. The true nature of the Constitution is not apparent on the surface, he said, for it contains no property qualifications for voting and does not outwardly recognize economic groups or confer special class privileges. Only if we study the newspapers and correspondence of the time, or read *The Federalist* or the debates in the Convention, do we begin to understand the true nature of the Constitution. Our understanding is broadened by a study of such items as the structure of government or the balance of power, powers conferred on the federal government and denied the state governments, and the economics of international politics. These will convince us, said Beard, that the Constitution was not a piece of abstract legislation reflecting no group

interests or economic antagonisms. It
was "an economic document drawn with
superb skill by men whose property interests were immediately at stake; and
as such it appealed directly and unerringly to identical interests in the country
at large" (p. 188).

We have already had occasion to note
Beard's questionable use of Madison and
The Federalist No. 10, but we need to
examine more fully his interpretation
of *The Federalist* in this chapter because
he relied much on this source for his
interpretation. Here, declared Beard, is
presented in relatively brief and systematic form an economic interpretation
of the Constitution by the men best qualified to expound the political science of
the new government. In fact, he said,
The Federalist was "the finest study in
the economic interpretation of politics
which exists in any language." When we
combine this with his previous opinion
that Madison's political philosophy in
No. 10 was "a masterly statement of the
theory of economic determinism in
politics" (p. 15), we begin to appreciate
Beard's concept of the importance of
The Federalist.

The first question to be answered then
is whether *The Federalist* presents merely
an "economic interpretation of politics."
Can Jay's arguments on the need for a
stronger union as protection from foreign
enemies, presented in Nos. 2 to 5, be
considered strictly economic? Was the
danger of civil war between the states,
as expounded by Hamilton, all due to
economic causes? Is an appeal for the
preservation of liberty and justice simply
an appeal to man's economic instincts?
Were all the criticisms of the Confederation and all the attempts to allay fears
about the form and powers of the new
government or freedom of the press
purely economic?

My answer to these questions is no,
and I have little doubt that anyone who
reads *The Federalist* without a propensity
for the economic interpretation of history
would find many noneconomic arguments
in this document. This is not to deny
that Hamilton, Madison, and Jay appealed to economic interests. On the contrary, there were many such appeals, as
there naturally would be to a people
the vast majority of whom were middle-
class property owners. But nationalism
and the fear of foreign domination can
have a much broader appeal than merely
the economic, and especially to a people
who have just emerged from under
British imperialism. We know there are
people who have some concern over
whether or not they have a voice in the
selection of their governors, a matter
certainly connected with the form of
government. There have been studies
showing that laboring men support their
unions not merely because the unions
work for better wages and hours, but
also because they help to give the worker
status as a human being. How much
simpler life would be if people did operate strictly from economic motives. . . .

We can use Madison to prove many
things, in addition to what Beard said
he proved. Given the Civil War, it would
be better to use him as a basis for a political philosophy of sectionalism rather
than economic class determinism.

Even if Beard had used [*The Federalist*]
No. 10 accurately, he would still have had
to show that it was more important to the
people at the time than the other eighty-
four numbers of *The Federalist*. Perhaps
some of the farmers actually believed that
a stronger government would benefit
them, as *The Federalist* suggested, by
opening up western lands for settlement
and by expanding the market for farm

products. Perhaps the artisans and mechanics believed that a stronger government would protect the sale of their
products by use of a tariff as they had
asked in their petitions and as *The Federalist* promised would happen. The fact
is that most of the people must have believed some of these arguments, for most
of them had the vote, and we can assume
that they did not vote for a government
which would promote only the interests
of personalty.

It follows from what has been said,
then, that the balance of powers, or
checks and balances, in the Constitution
were not there for the reasons attributed
by Beard. The Beard thesis follows the
line that personalty was under attack and
that it designed a system of checks and
balances by which the majority, presumably including the propertyless, the
debtors, and those with very little property, could not override the rights of the
minority—"which minority is of course
composed of those who possess property
that may be attacked" (p. 160). The way
to insure the rights of this minority, said
Beard, was to have a government in which
the different interests could check each
other and thus head off any pernicious
attacks. The House of Representatives,
he continued, came from those people
who were enfranchised, which did not
include the disfranchised "mass of men";
the Senate was elected by state legislatures which were themselves based on
property qualifications; and the president
was to be chosen by electors, which would
make him one step removed from the
electorate. Different terms of office for
each would make a complete overturn
in the government impossible at any
given time. Then the keystone of the
whole structure was a Supreme Court
which was not elected, which held office
during good behavior rather than at

pleasure, and which had the final power
of checking the other branches of the
government by declaring laws unconstitutional.

If the class structure was not what Beard
said it was, the corollary follows that
checks and balances were likewise not as
he pictured them. As I have already demonstrated, men in the Convention believed that there were all sorts of interests in the country, horizontal class
interests, vertical property groups, states'
rights, slave and free interests, and many
others. Of course it is true that checks
and balances were designed to allow these
different interests to restrain each other.
But we must remember that as recent
colonists, the people in 1787 had ex-
perienced a system of government in
which they did not have sufficient constitutional checks and balances. Even
Jefferson believed that the main fault
in the Virginia constitution was its failure
to provide checks to a legislative tyranny
by pitting different interests against each
other. As for the Senate's being elected
by state legislatures, we must remember
that one of the big issues in the Convention was whether the government was to
be national or federal, and those who
advocated a federal government insisted
that the Senate be elected by state legislatures to protect state interests. So while
some looked on the Senate as a safeguard
for property, others looked on it as the
branch which would represent the states.
Again, as I have said, some men did not
think the people would accept a national
government by giving up equal rights for
states in the Senate.

That the judiciary, as a "check," was
appointed during good behavior is not
unusual. In fact, the very reverse is true,
if we assume, as I do, that the Revolution
was designed primarily to keep the prevailing social order rather than to change

it. The colonies and states had long been accustomed to appointed judges. Furthermore, one of their strongest complaints against the British had come after 1760 when the British attempted to appoint judges during pleasure rather than during good behavior. The colonists had protested that their lives and property would not be safe in the hands of a judge who could be removed at the pleasure of the king.

And finally, the authors of *The Federalist* were not simply justifying checks and balances. What they had to do was to assure the people that the Constitution really provided for checks and balances, for its critics claimed that it did not do this. In fact, *The Federalist* pointed out that the Constitution had the same system of checks and balances that the state constitutions had, especially that of New York, which had one of the better systems of checks. One of the complaints of the colonists had been that they did not have checks on the British government, so checks and balances were nothing new.

A few quotations from the *Records* of the Convention will demonstrate what the members themselves thought of checks and balances. Madison said, as we have seen, that the landed interest dominated at the time; but in the future, when America resembled Europe, the landed interest would be outnumbered and it should have the power to check other interests. The North Carolina delegates believed that the Constitution was devised in such a way to protect the interests of North Carolina's citizens. Gerry agreed with Madison that the majority would violate justice if they had an interest in doing so, but he did not think there was any temptation for this in America because of cheap land. Charles Pinckney thought there were three groups, landed, professional, and commercial, that they were mutually depen-

dent on each other, and really had only one great interest in common. All that was needed, therefore, was to distribute powers of government in such a way as to provide a degree of permanency to the government—i.e. by checks and balances. Gerry said the people had two great interests—land and commerce (including stockholders). Since the people were chiefly composed of the landed interest, to draw both House and Senate from the people would not provide security for commerce. Wilson answered that the election of the Senate by state legislatures would not reduce the power of the landed interest, for landed interests controlled state legislatures and there was no reason to suppose that they would choose someone different for the Senate. Mason believed the purpose of the Convention was to devise a system that would obtain and preserve the protection, safety, and happiness of the people, and even Hamilton said the great question was the kind of government which would be best for the happiness of the country. King gave personal protection and security of property as one great object of government, while Hamilton said there were three concerns of government—agriculture, commerce, and revenue. There must be equality in the Senate to protect the small states, said Sherman, for states, like individuals, had their peculiar habits and usages. Madison even proposed a check and balance system between slave and free states, for he considered the conflict between them to be the main conflict in American society. "I do not, gentlemen, trust you," declared Bedford, and he went on to say that any group with power would probably abuse it, and that the small states must be protected from the large.

So there were many views of society expressed in the Convention and many reasons given for checks and balances besides the protection of property and especially personal property. We cannot simply take one delegate's view, and only one of his many opinions, and say "This represents the thinking of the Convention," as Beard did.

After disposing of these elements of the check and balance system, Beard went on to give the reasons why another check on democracy, property qualifications for voting and officeholding, was omitted from the Constitution. Again the reason was economic, not political, and Beard's argument runs as follows: The personalty interests represented in the Convention could not see any "safeguard at all in a freehold qualification against the assaults on vested personalty rights which had been made be the agrarians in every state." On the other hand, they could not have gotten a personalty qualification written into the Constitution even if they had desired. The reason: "there would have been no chance of securing a ratification of the Constitution at the hands of legislatures chosen by freeholders, or at the hands of conventions selected by them" (p. 166). Distrusting the freeholders and unable to get the kind of voting qualifications they wanted, these personalty interests preferred to omit all property qualifications from the Constitution. Beard hastened to add, however, that there was really "little risk to personalty" in leaving the question of voting qualifications to the states, for there were other checks in the Constitution itself and most of the states already had voting qualifications (p. 168). Thus is the omission of property qualifications from the Constitution explained in terms of personalty interests. . . .

The two reasons for the exclusion of property qualifications from the Constitution were political, not economic,

and they are not difficult to find in the *Records.*

One reason was that there were different qualifications in effect in different states and the delegates simply could not agree on a uniform qualification that would be satisfactory to all. Some wanted a freehold, others wanted to include any property, and a few would eliminate practically all qualifications. There was no great opposition to property qualifications for voting either in the Convention or in the country at large, for as Dickinson and Morris said, nine-tenths of the people were freeholders and would be pleased if voting were restricted to freeholders. But while most of the delegates favored a voting qualification, they could not agree on what that qualification should be. Ellsworth explained the situation as follows: "The different circumstances of different parts of the U.S. . . . render it improper to have either uniform or fixed qualifications. Wilson said it "was difficult to form any uniform rule of qualifications for all the states," and Rutledge said the committee considering the matter had omitted qualifications "because they could not agree on any among themselves."

The second reason for omitting property qualifications from the Constitution was also political—the delegates were simply afraid that any innovations on this point might result in the rejection of the Constitution. Wilson wanted to avoid "unnecessary innovations," while Ellsworth thought the prevailing state qualifications were sufficient, and that "the people [would] not readily subscribe to the Natl. Constitution, if it should subject them to be disfranchised." Men who wished for innovations on this point certainly were ignoring force of habit, declared Mason, for what would "the people say, if they should be disfranchised." Franklin did not want to displease the common people by disfranchising them, for they had contributed much during the late war. Sons of substantial farmers would not be pleased at being disfranchised, he said, and if the common people were "denied the right of suffrage it would debase their spirit and detach them from the interest of the country." Defending the habitual right of merchants and mechanics to vote, Gorham declared: "We must consult their rooted prejudices if we expect their concurrence in our propositions." Rutledge explained why the committee had omitted the qualifications by saying its members could not agree among themselves for fear of displeasing the people if they made the qualifications high or having the qualifications be worthless if they were low.

Since there were no personalty qualifications for voting in the Constitution, and since, as Beard said, the landed interests would control ratification either by state legislatures or by special conventions, the big question is this: Why was the Constitution ratified by the landed interests if it was designed to protect personalty? Beard never answered this question.

Inconsistencies and the drawing of unjustified conclusions soon become obvious when we attempt to follow the tortuous trail of the Beard thesis into the powers conferred on the federal government. Why did rural interests have to be conciliated on the point of direct taxes to prevent manufacturing states from shifting the tax burden to sparsely settled agricultural regions, if these rural regions were not represented in the Convention? Does the quotation from the North Carolina delegates (p. 169) prove the influence of personalty? No. The delegates said they had protected "the Southern states in general and North Carolina in particular" on the tax ques-

tion, but this represents a sectional or state interest, not personalty. These delegates were also looking out for the interests of North Carolina farmers, who, incidentally, had, on the average, land twice the value of that of the people in New England. And why did Hamilton have to conciliate "the freeholders and property owners in general" if the Convention represented personalty? Then there are the questions of whether military power and nationalism have nothing but economic connotations, even though everyone admits that economic factors accompany both.

One key to an understanding of the Constitutional Convention was provided by Beard himself in his discussion of the control of commerce (p. 175). His earlier use of petitions signed by mechanics and manufacturers was evidence that these skilled artisans wanted protection from foreign competition just as does organized labor today. But his final sentence in the paragraph is the important one—that merchants and manufacturing interests achieved commerical benefits, but "they paid for their victory by large concessions to the slave-owning planters of the south." This is only one example of what is so evident to anyone who reads the *Records* without preconceptions. There were a multitude of conflicting interests in the Convention, some economic and some not, and there simply had to be a great deal of compromising of interests for anything to be achieved. As one delegate said, he did not trust the other gentleman, and they all did everything possible to insure that their interests and principles got a hearing and that others' were checked as much as possible. Nobody could have his own way completely.

That the Constitution did not confer on Congress the power to make direct attacks on property is not to be wondered at (p. 176). Given the America of 1787, in which most men owned property, the reverse would have been the more astonishing. A constitution which permitted an attack on property would not have received a hearing in a country that had fought a revolution for the preservation of life, liberty, and property. One of the colonists' chief complaints against Britain had been that the British, on whom the colonists had no check, were endangering the property rights of colonists. The opponents of the Constitution were not opposed to the protection of property rights. After all, were not the Antifederalists responsible for the adoption of the first ten amendments, and did not Articles IV, V, and VII provide for additional protection of property which these Antifederalists did not think the Constitution provided?

If Madison was any authority, and Beard seemed to think he was, then Beard greatly exaggerated the importance of agrarianism in the country (pp. 178–79). Beard used the term, not to mean agricultural, but to designate men who favored an equal or a more nearly equal distribution of land. Madison stated in the Convention that as yet there had not been any agrarian attempts in the country.

Some interesting and significant points on obligation of contracts which Beard did not include in his discussion of the contract clause as a protection for personalty (pp. 179–83) were brought out in the *Records*. For instance, when King moved to add a clause prohibiting the states from interfering in private contracts, Gouverneur Morris objected. And his argument—shades of Oliver Wendell Holmes!—was that "within the State itself a majority must rule, whatever may be the mischief done among themselves." Even

Madison had his doubts about restricting the states on contracts, and Mason was strongly against it. Wilson then resolved the controversy with this answer: "The answer to these objections is that *retrospective* interferences only are to be prohibited." Instead of the original motion, then, the restriction was made that the state legislatures could not pass "retrospective laws," that is, ex post facto laws, and on this issue Connecticut, Maryland, and Virginia voted no. Later, however, Dickinson said he had examined Blackstone's *Commentaries on the Laws of England* and found that "ex post facto" related only to criminal cases, and that legislatures could still pass retrospective laws in civil cases. So the prohibition against violation of contracts was included, but to the members this meant only contracts already made. It did not in any way restrict the right of legislatures to provide the conditions under which future contracts could be made. . . .

The *Records* also gave a different version of paper money than that given by Beard, who implied that the adoption of the Constitution would put an end to paper money (pp. 178–80). He failed to point out that the adoption of restrictions against future emissions of paper money by the states did not annihilate paper money in the states or invalidate contracts that were to be paid in paper money. As Davie told the North Carolina convention: "The Federal Convention knew that several states had large sums of paper money in circulation, and that it was an interesting property, and they were sensible that those states would never consent to its immediate destruction, or ratify any system that would have that operation. The mischief already done could not be repaired: all that could be done was, to form some limitation to this great political evil. As the paper money had become private property, and the object of numberless contracts, it could not be destroyed or intermeddled with in that situation, although its baneful tendency was obvious and undeniable. It was, however, effecting an important object to put bounds to this growing mischief. If the states had been compelled to sink the paper money instantly, the remedy might be worse than the disease. As we could not put an immediate end to it, we were content with prohibiting its future increase, looking forward to its entire extinguishment when the states that had an emission circulating should be able to call it in by gradual redemption."

This puts the paper money restriction in quite a different light, just as the *Records* put the contract clause in a different light. State legislatures did not have to retire the paper money that was circulating, and contracts in paper money were still valid. As long as the paper money party controlled the state legislature, that party could keep bills of credit in circulation. Parties to contracts could still make contracts in paper money, even if the legislature could not make paper money a legal tender, and in the future both parties to a contract would know the conditions under which the contract was to be fulfilled. This, too, explains the lack of opposition to the bills of credit clause. Further research in a later period would show how long bills of credit circulated in the states and whether state legislatures did not, in effect, get around the Constitutional restriction by chartering state banks which issued bank notes, just as the colonists attempted to set up private land banks to replace the British-extinguished public banks.

In the last section of the chapter (pp. 183–88), Beard used Hamilton to prove a point that Hamilton did not prove, namely, that foreign and domestic controversies are based primarily on commercial antagonisms. What Hamilton appears to have been doing in *The Federalist* No. 6 was to convince the people that commerce was as important as other causes in the fomenting of wars. Hamilton was too realistic to make commerce the most important factor in war. The causes of hostility among nations were innumerable, he declared—love of power, desire of preeminence and dominion, desire for territory, jealousy of power, desire for equality and safety, and commercial rivalry, as well as private passions stemming from attachments, enmities, interests, hopes, and fears of leading individuals in their own communities. Even the caprices of women had caused wars. Sometimes countries engaged in wars contrary to their true interests, motivated by momentary passions and immediate interests rather than by general considerations of policy, utility, or justice. Men were subject to impulses of rage, resentment, jealousy, avarice, and other irregular and violent propensities. Was not the love of wealth as important a passion as love of power and glory, Hamilton asked? He implied that love of power and glory was important, and certainly he did not confine wealth to personalty. Hamilton did not rule out policy, utility, and justice as motivations, nor did he necessarily represent the views of other men in the Convention and the country at large.

So to prove that the Constitution was "an economic document drawn with superb skill by men whose property interests were immediately at stake," Beard had to violate the concepts of the historical method in many ways. These ran the gamut from omission to outright misrepresentation of evidence, and included the drawing of conclusions from evidence that not only did not warrant the conclusions but actually refuted them. To say that the Constitution was designed in part to protect property is true; to say that it was designed only to protect property is false; and to say that it was designed only to protect *personalty* is preposterous. . . .

The first feature of Beard's discussion of ratification to strike the reader is the fact that he did not take up the states in the order in which they ratified. Instead, he discussed them on somewhat of a geographical basis, starting with New Hampshire and going to Georgia, with the exception that he did place Rhode Island last. In Table II the reader can see at a glance the order used by Beard, together with the order in which the states actually ratified and the vote.

Why did Beard take up the states geographically instead of in the order in which they ratified? A geographical approach is irrelevant, since there is no correlation whatever between geography, the order of ratification, and the vote. On the other hand, a discussion of the states in the order in which they ratified would have been perfectly logical. Then we would have the same information that the people of the time had: that is, when Pennsylvania ratified, it was known that Delaware had ratified unanimously; and when Massachusetts ratified, everyone knew that five states had ratified, three unanimously and two by large majorities. But Beard did not choose to discuss the states in their logical order. We can never know why, but an analysis of the vote on ratification and experiments with students lead to some interesting speculations.

The reader's impression of the ease or difficulty of ratification depends on the order in which the states are discussed. I have found that students get the notion that ratification was easy if the states are

TABLE I

ORDER OF RATIFICATION	DATE OF RATIFICATION	VOTE ON RATIFICATION	
		FOR	AGAINST
1. Delaware	Dec. 7, 1787	30	0
2. Pennsylvania	Dec. 12, 1787	46	23
3. New Jersey	Dec. 18, 1787	39	0
4. Georgia	Jan. 2, 1788	26	0
5. Connecticut	Jan. 9, 1788	128	40
6. Massachusetts	Feb. 6, 1788	187	168
7. Maryland	April 28, 1788	63	11
8. South Carolina	May 23, 1788	149	73
9. New Hampshire	June 21, 1788	57	46
Vote after nine states had ratified		725	361
10. Virginia	June 25, 1788	89	79
11. New York	June 26, 1788	30	27
Vote of states forming Union when Washington took office, 1789		844	467
12. North Carolina	Nov. 21, 1789	—	—
13. Rhode Island	May 29, 1790	—	—

discussed in order of ease of ratification, with the easiest ratification first, and that it was difficult if the states are discussed in order of difficulty of ratification, with the most difficult ratification first. Beard's general interpretation was that the Constitution was put over by questionable methods only after a strenuous political battle. He started his discussion with New Hampshire and Massachusetts, the only two of the first nine where the vote was even remotely close, then skipped lightly over Connecticut to New York, a state where the vote was extremely close, but a state which was not even among the first nine to ratify. Not until the reader reaches New Jersey does he realize that the vote was not close in some states. But by then he has the impression that ratification was difficult in three out of the first four states, and he does not stop to see whether these were actually the first four states to ratify.

Had Beard taken up ratification in its logical order, that is, the order in which the states ratified, the reader might be tremendously impressed by the lack of opposition to the Constitution.

A glance at Table I gives a much different impression from that created by Beard with his account. Here we find that the vote in the first nine states to ratify was close in only two, Massachusetts and New Hampshire, or numbers six and nine respectively; that it was unanimous in three of the first four, Delaware, New Jersey, and Georgia; and that the margin of victory was overwhelming in the others. The total vote for the first nine ratifiers was 725 to 361, or 66.75 per cent to 33.25 per cent—a margin that would satisfy almost any politician—while the vote of the eleven states which put the Constitution in operation was 844 to 467, or a comfortable percentage of 64.37 to 35.63. This is not to deny that the vote in Massachusetts, New Hampshire, Virginia, and New York was fairly close, but it does place the vote of all the states in its proper perspective.

If the Beard thesis were correct—that the Constitution was put over by personalty and opposed by small farmers and debtors (realty)—one might expect to find some correlation between the quickness and ease with which the Constitution

TABLE II

ORDER IN WHICH BEARD DISCUSSED RATIFICATION	ORDER IN WHICH STATES RATIFIED	VOTE ON RATIFICATION	
		FOR	AGAINST
1. New Hampshire	9	57	46
2. Massachusetts	6	187	168
3. Connecticut	5	128	40
4. New York	11	30	27
5. New Jersey	3	39	0
6. Delaware	1	30	0
7. Pennsylvania	2	46	23
8. Maryland	7	63	11
9. Virginia	10	89	79
10. North Carolina	12	—	—
11. South Carolina	8	149	73
12. Georgia	4	26	0
13. Rhode Island	13	—	—

was ratified, on one hand, and the amount of realty and personality in the various states, on the other. To show this correlation, in Table III I have combined Table I with Beard's figures on realty and interest values (p. 36). My comparisons will show what can be done if generalizations are followed to their logical destinations. A few brief explanations will perhaps help the reader who is not statistically inclined.

The first five columns should be self-explanatory. They give the order and vote by which the states ratified, the amount of taxable land (not including houses) in the states, interest paid on the public debt in each state, and how this interest, which represents personality, compares with a state's realty.

Columns 6, 7, 8, and 9 are the important columns as far as correlations are concerned. Column 6 shows how the states should have ratified if there is a close correlation between the speed with which states ratified and the amount of opposition in the state. In short, the states with the least opposition to the Constitution should have ratified soonest and by the largest vote, and on this score there is a fair correlation.

Column 7 shows how the states should have ratified if there was a close relationship between land values and ratification. If the opposition came from agriculture, we might expect to find states with the least value in land ratifying first while those with the most land would ratify last. The correlation is perfect for Delaware, almost completely reversed for Rhode Island and Pennsylvania, fair for Georgia, Maryland, Virginia, and New York, but not very close for the others.

From the standpoint of the Beard thesis, columns 8 and 9 are the most important. Here we have the way the states should have ratified on the basis of total inter-

est paid and the way interest compared with realty. If interest represented securities, those states receiving the most interest should have ratified the most quickly and easily, as should also those states where interest formed the largest percentage of total wealth. The correlation in column 8 is not very significant. Connecticut and North Carolina are perfect, but Delaware is completely reversed and Georgia is off considerably, while New York and Massachusetts, where the vote was close, should have been the first two to ratify. Similarly, the correlation in column 9 has little significance. South Carolina, Massachusetts, New York and Rhode Island should have ratified first but actually ranked well down the list. New Jersey, Delaware, and Georgia rank among the last four but were among the first four to ratify.

If we use as a basis for correlation the per capita figures for land values and interest disbursed instead of total values (Table IV), there is no significant correlation, again assuming that the states with the largest per capita realty would have opposed the Constitution and those with the largest per capita interest would have favored it. On land values, Massachusetts correlates perfectly and Delaware, New Hampshire, and New York are close, but the other states are almost reversed. Elimination of slaves would raise the per capita value of land for whites in the southern states but probably would not change the order very much. On the basis of interest disbursed, the correlation is perfect for Virginia, New Hampshire, and Connecticut, and close for Maryland and North Carolina. But it is almost reversed for New York, Rhode Island, Georgia, and Delaware. Georgia and Virginia had the same per capita interest, $0.08 yet one ratified quickly and unanimously while the other ratified late

TABLE III

COMPARISON OF RATIFICATION, LAND VALUES, AND INTEREST DISBURSED

States by order of ratification (1)	Vote on ratification (2)	Valuation of land, not including $140,000,000 for houses (3)	Interest disbursed, presumably on public debt (4)	Percentage of interest disbursed to total value of land and interest (5)	States by order of ease of ratification (6)	Order in which states should have ratified on basis of land values (7)	Order in which states should have ratified on basis of interest disbursed (8)	Order in which states should have ratified on basis of percentage of interest to total (9)
1. Delaware	30–0	$ 4,053,248	$ 2,980	0.074	1. N.J.	1. Del.	1. N.Y.	1. S.C.
2. Pennsylvania	46–23	72,824,852	86,379	0.119	2. Del.	2. R.I.	2. Mass.	2. Mass.
3. New Jersey	39–0	27,287,981	27,350	0.101	3. Ga.	3. Ga.	3. S.C.	3. N.Y.
4. Georgia	26–0	10,263,506	6,800	0.067	4. Md.	4. S.C.	4. Penn.	4. R.I.
5. Connecticut	128–40	40,163,955	79,600	0.198	5. Conn.	5. N.H.	5. Conn.	5. Md.
6. Massachusetts	187–168	54,445,642	309,500	0.573	6. S.C.	6. Md.	6. Md.	6. Conn.
7. Maryland	63–11	21,634,004	74,000	0.341	7. Penn.	7. N.J.	7. Va.	7. Penn.
8. South Carolina	149–73	12,456,720	109,500	0.872	8. N.H.	8. N.C.	8. R.I.	8. Va.
9. New Hampshire	57–46	19,028,108	20,000	0.105	9. Va.	9. Conn.	9. N.J.	9. N.H.
10. Virginia	86–79	59,976,860	63,300	0.106	10. Mass.	10. Mass.	10. N.H.	10. N.J.
11. New York	30–27	74,885,075	367,600	0.489	11. N.Y.	11. Va.	11. Ga.	11. Del.
12. North Carolina	–	27,909,479	3,200	0.012	12. N.C.	12. Penn.	12. N.C.	12. Ga.
13. Rhode Island	–	8,082,355	31,700	0.391	13. R.I.	13. N.Y.	13. Del.	13. N.C.

TABLE IV

PER CAPITA VALUES OF LAND AND INTEREST DISBURSED

States by order of ratification	Population in 1790, including slaves	Per capita value of land not including $140,000,000 for houses	Per capita value of interest disbursed	Order in which states should have ratified on basis of per capita land values	Order in which states should have ratified on basis of interest per capita
1. Delaware	59,096	$ 68.41	$0.05	1. S.C.	1. N.Y.
2. Pennsylvania	434,373	121.61	0.20	2. Md.	2. Mass.
3. New Jersey	184,139	159.05	0.15	3. Del.	3. R.I.
4. Georgia	82,548	124.33	0.08	4. N.C.	4. S.C.
5. Connecticut	237,946	168.79	0.34	5. Va.	5. Conn.
6. Massachusetts	475,327	114.56	0.65	6. Mass.	6. Md.
7. Maryland	319,728	67.66	0.23	7. R.I.	7. Penn.
8. South Carolina	249,073	50.01	0.44	8. Penn.	8. N.J.
9. New Hampshire	141,885	134.10	0.14	9. Ga.	9. N.H.
10. Virginia	747,610	80.22	0.08	10. N.H.	10. Va.
11. New York	340,120	220.17	1.08	11. N.J.	11. Ga.
12. North Carolina	393,751	70.88	0.01	12. Conn.	12. Del.
13. Rhode Island	68,825	117.43	0.46	13. N.Y.	13. N.C.

and by a close vote. New York and Virginia both ratified late and by a close vote, but they were completely unlike in security holding.

For all practical purposes there is no correlation between ratification, on the one hand, and realty and personalty, on the other.

Still another element in the Beard technique should be noted in relation to his discussion of ratification. This was the relatively large amount of space he gave to states where ratification was close or the methods were questionable, and the small amount of space he accorded to the states which ratified unanimously or by overwhelming majorities. For an understanding of the Constitution, it seems to me that we need to know not only why the vote was close in some states, but also why it was not close in seven of the first eleven to ratify. . . .

In line with his thesis, Beard attempted to show through his discussion of the popular vote on the Constitution that the Constitution did not result from what we consider the democratic process. By now, of course, the reader realizes the danger of interpreting the Constitution as the product of an undemocratic society, but we still need to examine this chapter to see how Beard has used his evidence and arrived at his conclusions.

We need to dwell for a moment on Beard's contention that the question of holding a convention was not submitted to popular vote and was not an issue in the election of legislatures which selected the delegates. A popular election of a convention to amend the Articles of Confederation would have been unthinkable in 1787. In the first place, it would have been unconstitutional, for the Articles set up a federation which could act only on states, not on individuals, and a popular election of a convention to alter the Articles would have been out of the question. The calling of the Constitutional Convention by state legislatures was perfectly legal under the Articles: the departure from legal processes came when the delegates abandoned their instructions to amend the Articles, adopted a new system, and then had it ratified by conventions rather than state legislatures. As far as I have been able to tell, the people in 1787 were about as agitated over the fact that they did not elect the delegates to the Constitutional Convention as the American people are in 1955 that they do not elect this country's delegates to the United Nations.

Neither was it unusual that the Constitution was not submitted to popular ratification. The calling of the First Continental Congress had not been submitted to popular vote; the calling of the Second Continental Congress had not been submitted to popular vote; the Declaration of Independence had not been submitted to popular vote; and the Articles of Confederation had not been submitted to popular vote. With this precedent, why would we expect the ratification of the Constitution to deviate from accepted practice? In fact, Mason in the Convention argued that ratification by nine states would be acceptable to the people because all important questions under the Confederation had required the consent of nine states, and he "was for preserving ideas familiar to the people." The other states supported Mason's motion 8 to 3, so other men must have thought the same.

As usual, the *Records* supply the answer to the question of popular ratification of the Constitution. For one thing, the delegates seem to have thought that ratification of the Constitution by conventions expressly chosen by the people for that purpose was ratification by the people. When the Convention considered the

resolution calling for ratification by state conventions, many delegates expressed opinions which would indicate that they considered this method to be practically the same as a popular referendum. George Mason "considered a reference of the plan to the authority of the people as one of the most important and essential of the Resolutions. The Legislatures have no power to ratify it. . . . Whither then must we resort? To the people with whom all power remains that has not been given up in the Constitutions derived from them." Gerry opposed because "great confusion he was confident would result from a recurrence to the people." Ellsworth explained it this way: "As to the 1st. point, he observed that a new sett of ideas seemed to have crept in since the articles of Confederation were established. Conventions of the people, or with power derived expressly from the people, were not then thought of. The Legislatures were considered competent. Their ratification has been acquiesced in without complaint." We might easily say that ratification by conventions elected expressly for that purpose was as radical an approach as the initiative and referendum were in 1913.

When we get to Beard's discussion of the voters themselves (p. 240), we again encounter that horrible specter, the disfranchised. . . . All we need to note here is that Beard dragged him forth again when he contended that "a considerable portion of the adult white male population was debarred from participating in the elections of delegates to the ratifying conventions by the prevailing property qualifications on the suffrage."

After citing the qualifications for the election of ratifying conventions (the same as the qualifications for election of state representatives, except in Connecticut, where all voters in town meetings were enfranchised, and in New York, where manhood suffrage prevailed) Beard answered his own question about how many men were disfranchised. He said "that only about 3 per cent of the population dwelt in towns of over 8000 inhabitants in 1790, and that freeholds were widely distributed, especially in New England." We have already seen that a larger percentage of the population in North Carolina than in New England were freeholders and that their land was on the average worth twice as much as the freeholders' land in New England. If, as I contend, a farmer could not have made a living on a freehold small enough to disfranchise him, Beard is really saying here that most men were farmers and therefore qualified voters. His other evidence from sources will support this generalization, not only for farmers but for "city" dwellers as well.

Actually, Beard confused the issue by his statement that "far more were disfranchised through apathy and lack of understanding of the significance of politics" (p. 242). In the first place, a man is not "disfranchised" if he has the right to vote but does not use it. The term disfranchised means that he has been deprived of the right, not that he simply failed to exercise his right. In the second place, the problems of whether a man *can* vote, but does not, are quite different from those of whether he *cannot* vote, but wants to.

When he stopped talking about those who *could not* vote and started talking about those who *did not* vote, Beard was on sound historical ground from the standpoint of historical method. One of the master keys to an understanding of the Constitution is not how many men could not vote, but why so many having

the vote did not use it. Beard used evidence that is absolutely correct when he generalized about the "noteworthy fact that only a small proportion of the population entitled to vote took the trouble to go to the polls until the hot political contests of the Jeffersonian era." When we stop talking about the "mass of men" who *could not* vote on the Constitution and start talking about the "mass of men" who *could* vote but did not bother to do so, then, and only then, will we understand the Constitution and its adoption.

Beard unwittingly gave the answer to this political apathy. On page 242 he implied that the journey to the polls and delays at elections were troublesome, thus accounting for the smallness of the vote. This had little to do with the problem. The governing factor was whether or not there was an issue, or whether the people thought there was an issue, and how important it was. Beard gave figures to show that few people in Massachusetts voted in 1786, before Shays' Rebellion, but that in 1787, after Shays' Rebellion, the number trebled. This is correct, and anyone can chart the importance of the issues of the day by checking on the vote. In other words, the people exercised their right to vote when they thought something was at stake, and failed to vote when they were not particularly interested. . . .

Since Beard himself admitted that a careful study of South Carolina could give an accurate picture of the vote in that state . . . , his attempt to suggest that the opposition vote there may well have represented a majority is simply guesswork. In fact, he had previously made the point (p. 238) that the popular vote in South Carolina had never been figured out. Until it is, all we are justified in saying is that the state ratified by a convention vote of more than two to one after the people had been given the whole winter and spring to consider the Constitution.

Another example of an unwarranted conclusion from the evidence presented appears in the paragraph in the middle of page 249. The evidence is that in the election of 1788 the vote was only 2.8 per cent of the population in New Hampshire, 2.7 per cent in Madison's district in Virginia, 3.6 per cent in Maryland, and 3 per cent in Massachusetts. These figures mean only that few people were sufficiently concerned to exercise their right to vote. Yet out of this kind of evidence, Charles Oscar Paullin conjured, and Beard accepted without criticism, the following conclusion: "'The voting was done chiefly by a small minority of interested property holders, a disproportionate share of whom in the northern states resided in the towns, and the wealthier and more talented of whom like a closed corporation controlled politics.'" The evidence does not justify this conclusion under a proper use of historical method. One is reminded of the lawyer who told the jury: "Out of these conclusions I draw my facts."

Given all this discussion, we can only conclude that Beard's estimates of the total vote on the Constitution are mere guesses (p. 250). Since we do not know how many people voted, we are not justified in saying that 100,000 voted for it and 60,000 voted against it. But if we did accept those figures, we could say that 62.5 per cent of those who voted favored the Constitution and 37.5 per cent opposed it, which is a substantial majority. Franklin D. Roosevelt received only 62.22 per cent of the popular vote in 1936, but I am sure most people would consider this a smashing victory in American politics.

As for the men who did not vote, we can only conjecture about their views on the Constitution. If they had held strong opinions one way or the other, they probably would have gone to the polls. A logical assumption would be that the actual vote was a fairly close representation of the views of the total voting population, and that if every man had voted, the result would not have been much different from what it was, except in number. At any rate, democracy means a majority of those who vote, at least until we have compulsory voting, and there can be little doubt that the Constitution received that majority. . . .

Instead of the Beard interpretation that the Constitution was put over undemocratically in an undemocratic society by personal property, the following fourteen paragraphs are offered as a possible interpretation of the Constitution and as suggestions for future research on that document.

1. The movement for the Constitution was originated and carried through by men who had long been important in both economic and political affairs in their respective states. Some of them owned personalty, more of them owned realty, and if their property was adversely affected by conditions under the Articles of Confederation, so also was the property of the bulk of the people in the country, middle-class farmers as well as town artisans.

2. The movement for the Constitution, like most important movements, was undoubtedly started by a small group of men. They were probably interested personally in the outcome of their labors, but the benefits which they expected were not confined to personal property or, for that matter, strictly to things economic. And if their own interests would be enhanced by a new government,

similar interests of other men, whether agricultural or commercial, would also be enhanced.

3. Naturally there was no popular vote on the calling of the convention which drafted the Constitution. Election of delegates by state legislatures was the constitutional method under the Articles of Confederation, and had been the method long established in this country. Delegates to the Albany Congress, the Stamp Act Congress, the First Continental Congress, the Second Continental Congress, and subsequent congresses under the Articles were all elected by state legislatures, not by the people. Even the Articles of Confederation had been sanctioned by state legislatures, not by popular vote. This is not to say that the Constitutional Convention should not have been elected directly by the people, but only that such a procedure would have been unusual at the time. Some of the opponents of the Constitution later stressed, without avail, the fact that the Convention had not been directly elected. But at the time the Convention met, the people in general seemed to be about as much concerned over the fact that they had not elected the delegates as the people of this country are now concerned over the fact that they do not elect our delegates to the United Nations.

4. Present evidence seems to indicate that there were no "propertyless masses" who were excluded from the suffrage at the time. Most men were middle-class farmers who owned realty and were qualified voters, and, as the men in the Convention said, mechanics had always voted in the cities. Until credible evidence proves otherwise, we can assume that state legislatures were fairly representative at the time. We cannot condone the fact that a few men were probably disfranchised by prevailing property qualifications, but it makes a great deal

of difference to an interpretation of the Constitution whether the disfranchised comprised ninety-five per cent of the adult men or only five per cent. Figures which give percentages of voters in terms of the entire population are misleading, since less than twenty per cent of the people were adult men. And finally, the voting qualifications favored realty, not personalty.

5. If the members of the Convention were directly interested in the outcome of their work and expected to derive benefits from the establishment of the new system, so also did most of the people of the country. We have many statements to the effect that the people in general expected substantial benefits from the labors of the Convention.

6. The Constitution was not just an economic document, although economic factors were undoubtedly important. Since most of the people were middle-class and had private property, practically everybody was interested in the protection of property. A constitution which did not protect property would have been rejected without any question, for the American people had fought the Revolution for the preservation of life, liberty, and property. Many people believed that the Constitution did not go far enough to protect property, and they wrote these views into the amendments to the Constitution. But property was not the only concern of those who wrote and ratified the Constitution, and we would be doing a grave injustice to the political sagacity of the Founding Fathers if we assumed that property or personal gain was their only motive.

7. Naturally the delegates recognized that the protection of property was important under government, but they also recognized that personal rights were equally important. In fact, persons and property were usually bracketed together

as the chief objects of government protection.

8. If three-fourths of the adult males failed to vote on the election of delegates to ratifying conventions, this fact signified indifference, not disfranchisement. We must not confuse those who could *not* vote with those who *could* vote but failed to exercise their right. Many men at the time bewailed the fact that only a small portion of the voters ever exercised their prerogative. But this in itself should stand as evidence that the conflict over the Constitution was not very bitter, for if these people had felt strongly one way or the other, more of them would have voted.

Even if we deny the evidence which I have presented and insist that American society was undemocratic in 1787, we must still accept the fact that the men who wrote the Constitution believed that they were writing it for a democratic society. They did not hide behind an iron curtain of secrecy and devise the kind of conservative government that they wanted without regard to the views and interests of "the people." More than anything else, they were aware that "the people" would have to ratify what they proposed, and that therefore any government which would be acceptable to the people must of necessity incorporate much of what was customary at the time. The men at Philadelphia were practical politicians, not political theorists. They recognized the multitude of different ideas and interests that had to be reconciled and compromised before a constitution would be acceptable. They were far too practical, and represented far too many clashing interests themselves, to fashion a government weighted in favor of personalty or to believe that the people would adopt such a government.

9. If the Constitution was ratified by a vote of only one-sixth of the adult men, that again demonstrates indifference and not disfranchisement. Of the one-fourth of the adult males who voted, nearly two-thirds favored the Constitution. Present evidence does not permit us to say what the popular vote was except as it was measured by the votes of the ratifying conventions.

10. Until we know what the popular vote was, we cannot say that it is questionable whether a majority of the voters in several states favored the Constitution. Too many delegates were sent uninstructed. Neither can we count the towns which did not send delegates on the side of those opposed to the Constitution. Both items would signify indifference rather than sharp conflict over ratification.

11. The ratifying conventions were elected for the specific purpose of adopting or rejecting the Constitution. The people in general had anywhere from several weeks to several months to decide the question. If they did not like the new government, or if they did not know whether they liked it, they could have voted *no* and there would have been no Constitution. Naturally the leaders in the ratifying conventions represented the same interests as the members of the Constitutional Convention—mainly realty and some personalty. But they also represented their constituents in these same interests, especially realty.

12. If the conflict over ratification had been between substantial personalty interests on the one hand and small farmers and debtors on the other, there would not have been a constitution. The small farmers comprised such an overwhelming percentage of the voters that they could have rejected the new government without any trouble. Farmers and debtors are not synonymous terms and should

not be confused as such. A town-by-town or county-by-county record of the vote would show clearly how the farmers voted.

13. The Constitution was created about as much by the whole people as any government could be which embraced a large area and depended on representation rather than on direct participation. It was also created in part by the states, for as the *Records* show, there was strong state sentiment at the time which had to be appeased by compromise. And it was created by compromising a whole host of interests throughout the country, without which compromises it could never have been adopted.

14. If the intellectual historians are correct, we cannot explain the Constitution without considering the psychological factors also. Men are motivated by what they believe as well as by what they have. Sometimes their actions can be explained on the basis of what they hope to have or hope that their children will have. Madison understood this fact when he said that the universal hope of acquiring property tended to dispose people to look favorably upon property. It is even possible that some men support a given economic system when they themselves have nothing to gain by it. So we would want to know what the people in 1787 thought of their class status.

Did workers and small farmers believe that they were lower-class, or did they, as many workers do now, consider themselves middle-class? Were the common people trying to eliminate the Washingtons, Adamses, Hamiltons, and Pinckneys, or were they trying to join them?

As did Beard's fourteen conclusions, these fourteen suggestions really add up to two major propositions: the Constitution was adopted in a society which was fundamentally democratic, not undemocratic; and it was adopted by a people who were primarily middle-class property owners, especially farmers who owned realty, not just by the owners of personalty. At present these points seem to be justified by the evidence, but if better evidence in the future disproves or modifies them, we must accept that evidence and change our interpretation accordingly.

After this critical analysis, we should at least not begin future research on this period of American history with the illusion that the Beard thesis of the Constitution is valid. If historians insist on accepting the Beard thesis in spite of this analysis, however, they must do so with the full knowledge that their acceptance is founded on "an act of faith," not an analysis of historical method, and that they are indulging in a "noble dream," not history.

BENJAMIN FLETCHER WRIGHT (1900–   ) is
president emeritus of Smith College. Now retired from
academic life, he lives in his native Texas. In this
selection, taken from his 1957 Bacon Lectures at Boston
University, Wright contends that the Constitution was
possible only because of the agreement of the framers
and most Americans on the basic outline of what was
needed in a new government. Those issues which
required considerable deliberation and compromise
were economic quarrels between North and South, not
between creditors and debtors or merchants and
farmers.*

Benjamin Fletcher Wright

Government-Making by Consensus

No one could possibly defend the
proposition that the Constitution does
not embody a considerable number of
compromises. The question is whether
this sweeping statement is an accurate and
meaningful interpretation of what took
place in the Federal Convention. Few of
the hundreds who have written about that
remarkable group have attempted to draw
discriminating conclusions about the
nature and basic reasons for agreement
and disagreement during its meetings.
Among the most interesting and useful
generalizations I have discovered are
those found in Robert Livingston Schuyler's little book, *The Constitution of the
United States.* He concluded that "the
disputes in the Convention, the occasions
for compromise, were many, but most of
them arose over questions essentially
political. If one approaches the work of
the Convention from the point of view
of government and political science,
he will naturally be impressed by its
compromises. But on the great economic
questions at issue between debtor and
creditor, farmer and merchant, there
was little need for compromise, for there
was little disagreement among the delegates."[1] The distinctions between political and economic disagreement and
agreement suggests the possibility of an
analysis more inclusive, as well as more
incisive, than the customary one-sentence
generalization.

In my analysis of this problem I shall

[1] *The Constitution of the United States* (New York,
1923), pp. 111–112

first deal with disagreement and compromise, and then discuss the nature and importance of agreement. A discussion of disagreement and compromise may properly begin with the first and major obstacle to the success of the Convention, the issue of representation in Congress. The Convention was the last time in American history when the large states were lined up on one side and the small states on the other. The latter group, or most of them, insisted on equality of representation in Congress so that each state would, as in the Stamp Act Congress, the First and Second Continental Congresses, and the Congress under the Articles of Confederation, have an equal vote. To us this division seems largely artificial, but it reflected strongly held views in 1787. For a time the disagreement over it threatened to disrupt the Convention. Out of that disagreement came the major compromise by which equality of representation was provided for the Senate, while in the House the states were to be represented in accordance with their population. After this compromise had been adopted the large state, small state line-up disappeared, only to reappear briefly when the problem of electing a President came up. Of course the equality of representation in the Senate, according to which at the present time New York and Nevada each have two senators, has been an important factor in American history, as in the decades preceding the Civil War, but the basis of division has rarely, if ever, been the size of the states.

Another issue relating to representation in Congress was involved in the counting of slaves. Those states in which there were many slaves wished them to be counted for purposes of representation. The result of this particular disagreement was the provision that three-fifths of the slaves shall be counted. So

close a student of the Convention as Professor Schuyler argues that the three-fifths clause was "not the result of a compromise," because "there was nothing new about it."[2] It is true that the principle of counting three-fifths of the slaves had been found in an amendment proposed to the Articles of Confederation and the same principle was proposed in the New Jersey Plan. But it is also true that this is an issue on which members of the Convention disagreed, and that the three-fifths ratio was a compromise between those who wished to have slaves counted and those who wished to have them not counted. Had they been a little more logical, perhaps they would have agreed on a fifty-fifty division, but they simply took over the three-fifths ratio as it had been proposed under the Articles.

The qualifications for voting was a subject over which there was disagreement in the Convention, some delegates favoring a property qualification, others being opposed. The Convention decided to leave the regulation of the suffrage to the several states, largely because there were such varying regulations among them. The tendency during and after the Revolution was toward liberalizing the suffrage, a tendency with which the Federal Convention did not attempt to interfere, much less to block. There was apparently no serious disagreement when the delegates decided not to follow the example of most of the states and to require neither property nor religious qualifications for office holding.

One of the clearest examples we have of disagreement and compromise concerns the term of office of members of both houses of Congress. The terms finally agreed upon, two years for members of the House and six for members of the Senate, were clearly the results of

---

[2] *The Constitution of the United States,* p. 103.

compromises, since almost everything was proposed at one time or another, from a one-year term for Representatives, to a life term for Senators.

In view of the important part played in the calling of the Convention by the weakness of the government under the Articles and its inability to carry on the ordinary functions of government, it is surprising how little time was devoted to the discussion, except perhaps in committees, of whose proceedings we have no record, of the powers granted to Congress. The Virginia Plan contained an extremely broad and general grant of powers. There was some discussion of this proposal with indications of disagreement, but the enumeration of the powers of Congress, largely as we find it in the Constitution today, came from the Committee on Detail. A few of the powers proposed, either by that Committee or by individual members of the Convention, were voted down, e.g., the power to issue charters of incorporation, and the power to emit bills of credit, but otherwise opposition to specific powers of Congress was largely in terms of sectional or regional jealousies and fears.

The power to regulate commerce, together with the power to levy customs duties, seems to have been generally accepted, but the delegates from South Carolina and Georgia were bitterly opposed to allowing Congress to regulate, perhaps to abolish, the slave trade. All of the southern states were opposed to the imposition of any tax on exports, since the agrarian South was then the principal exporting area of the country. A majority of the states seems to have been in favor of allowing Congress to abolish the slave trade, but the three southern states indicated that they would stay out of the union if such a power were entrusted to Congress. As a result Con-

gress was prohibited from forbidding the importation of slaves before 1808, and was permitted to impose a tax on "such importation, not exceeding ten dollars for each person." The Congress was also forbidden to impose export taxes. The South won on both of these issues.

On the regulation of foreign commerce or, to use the term most frequently employed in the Convention, "navigation laws," the South wanted protection against regulations which would discriminate against that section, and tried to secure adoption of a requirement that such statutes could be enacted only by a two-thirds vote of both houses of Congress. This they failed to obtain; on this part of the general question of the regulation of commerce the South lost.

The southern states were also fearful of discriminatory action by the Congress when it came to the levying of direct taxes. The term "direct tax" in 1787 apparently did not include income taxes but was rather thought of as limited to taxes on land measured by area and on persons by number. The compromise here was similar to the compromise on counting slaves in representation. Direct taxes were prohibited unless they were apportioned among the states by population, counting three-fifths of the slaves for this purpose.

When the Virginia Plan was introduced it was made clear that the representatives from that powerful state wished to give to the national Congress the power to veto all laws "contravening in the opinion of the National Legislature the articles of Union." That is in sharp contrast with the system then existing, though it has a clear similarity to the power exercised by the Board of Trade over the several colonial legislatures. It is, however, less extreme than Hamilton's proposal that the veto be vested in the governors of the states, since the governors were to be appointed by the national government. Hamilton's suggestion was not seriously considered, but the provision of the Virginia Plan was reported out favorably by the Committee on the Whole. By that time, however, more anti-nationalist representatives were present and it soon became evident that the Virginia proposal was not acceptable to many of the delegates. It is one of the paradoxes of the Federal Convention that the Supreme Law clause of Article VI, which has, at least since the time of Chief Justice Marshall, been generally recognized as one of the bulwarks of national power, originated in the New Jersey Plan and was inserted in the Constitution after being reproposed on July 17 by Luther Martin of Maryland. Luther Martin was one of those most opposed to centralization; he refused to agree with the Constitution as drafted and he was among the most ardent and most vocal of Anti-Federalists. But when he proposed the Supreme Law clause on July 17, it was agreed to without debate or opposition. Much later, on August 23, Pinckney proposed a legislative veto, one requiring a two-thirds vote of Congress, but this lost by a vote of five states to six.

Contrary to some uninformed opinion about the Convention, there was no debate over the broad issue which became so important in the latter part of the nineteenth century and is among the central issues of the present day, laissez-faire versus collectivism. They neither debated, accepted, nor rejected individualism, the welfare state, or socialism.

The sections of the Constitution dealing with the national legislative body were not the only ones which were the basis for differences of opinion and for compromises. A number of the provisions relating to the executive department of the government, most of which are to be found in Article II of the Constitution, were debated and several are the result of compromises. The clearest instance of this is to be found in the numerous discussions and votes relating to the election of the President.

It will be remembered that the Articles of Confederation provided for no national executive as we understand that term. There was a President of Congress, but he was little more than a presiding officer of the legislative branch. There was also a Committee of the States but it and other committees were not independent of the Congress. There was of course no precedent for the election of an executive. It was quickly agreed in the Convention that there should be a separate executive, but it took them more than three months to agree upon a method of election.

If there was no national executive under the Articles of Confederation, there were separate executives in all of the states, one-man executives in all except Pennsylvania. Only three of the states (New York, Massachusetts, and New Hampshire) provided for popular election of the governor. In the others the state executive was elected by the state legislature. It is therefore not surprising that the Virginia Plan called for election of the national executive by Congress. That seemed the most obvious method, as well as the one in accordance with the practice in three-fourths of the states. That principle of election was generally favored during most of the summer, and on at least one occasion it seems to have been approved by unanimous vote of the states present. Nevertheless, the delegates had doubts about it and when, on August 31, a committee consisting of one delegate from each state was appointed to deal with parts of the Constitution not acted on or postponed, the method of electing the President was one of the problems submitted to it. Apparently one of the reasons why there had been something less than complete agreement was that the smaller states wanted equality of voting in the selection of the President. This committee reported out our curious method of electing a President. It combines features from almost all of the proposals made up to that time, though it is also to be said that it is very similar to a proposal made nearly three months earlier by James Wilson. This compromise plan provided for election by an electoral college, the state legislatures to decide on the method by which the electors were to be selected in each state, the number of electors to be equal to the number of representatives in the House and Senate combined. If no candidate should receive a majority of the votes cast, something which the Founding Fathers thought would be frequently the case, the Senate was to elect from the five candidates standing highest, or from the top two if they were tied, both having a majority, as was possible under a system according to which each elector would vote for two candidates, one of whom could not be a citizen of the elector's state. On the floor of the Convention this system was slightly changed, the principal alteration being that a runoff election would take place in the House rather than the Senate, but, as a concession to the small states, each state would have a single vote.

The Convention went along happily for over three months without anyone suggesting that the country needed a Vice President. That office was proposed by the committee which offered the compromise method of electing the President and, when a question was raised about

the need for a Vice President, there was but a single answer, that the committee introduced this office "for the sake of a valuable mode of election which requires two to be chosen at the same time." This answer was based upon the assumption that the electors would vote, to the extent possible, for favorite sons of their own states. But it remains a strange reason for the introduction of an officer given but one duty, that of presiding over the Senate, and, if I may quote former Vice President Marshall, a single obligation, that of inquiring each day about the health of the President, since the compromise plan also called for the succession of the Vice President to "the powers and duties of the said office" when that office becomes vacant "in case of the removal of the President from office, or of his death, resignation, or inability to discharge the powers and duties of the said office."

So long as the delegates were of the opinion that the President should be elected by Congress, they favored a single term, probably of seven years. Apparently they were afraid that he would be dependent upon Congress if he had to look to the Congress for re-election. With the acceptance of the compromise method for the election of the President the term was changed to one of four years and nothing was said about re-eligibility.

The views concerning the relation of the President to Congress[3] varied from that expressed by Roger Sherman on June 1 to that expressed by Alexander Hamilton on June 18. Neither of these was at all representative of the Conven-

---

[3] On this and other issues related to the separation of powers see my article, "The Origins of the Separation of Powers in America," *Economica* (London), May, 1933, pp. 169–185.

tion. Sherman said, "He considered the Executive Magistracy as nothing more than an institution for carrying the will of the Legislature into effect, that the person or persons ought to be appointed by and accountable to the Legislature only, which was the depositary of the supreme will of the Society." It is doubtful if anyone, except perhaps Franklin, agreed with this view, and Sherman changed his mind during the course of the summer.

The other extreme is found in Hamilton's plan and speech, since he wished a "supreme executive authority" to be vested in a single officer who shall be elected "to serve during good behavior," i.e., for life or unless earlier removed, this executive to be elected by electors chosen by the people in election districts. In addition to having life tenure, the executive would exercise great independent power, including an absolute veto over acts of Congress.

The most representative point of view and the one which was nearest to that accepted by the Convention, was expressed at various times by James Madison. It may be noted that both James Wilson and Gouverneur Morris wanted an even stronger executive than did Madison, or than did the majority of the delegates.

The powers allocated to the executive were the result of much discussion and some compromises. There were also a number of proposals which were simply voted down, with no resulting compromises. The absolute veto, for example, was proposed at least three times, but was always defeated. The committee report which proposed the compromise method of electing the President, increased the powers of that officer by adding the authority to negotiate treaties and to make important appointments with the advice and consent of the Senate. The change meant a considerable increase of executive authority; previously both powers had been assigned to the Senate alone. The committee also inserted the provision which is the sole constitutional basis for the Cabinet, that the President could require the opinions in writing of the heads of the several departments.

This survey of the work of the Convention supports Professor Schuyler's interpretation in part, but only in part. It is true that "the disputes in the Convention, the occasions for compromise, were many, but most of them arose over questions essentially political." Moreover, the absence of any lengthy or serious dispute over the prohibitions upon state power contained in Section 10 of Article I—those prohibiting the states from coining money, emitting bills of credit, making anything but gold and silver coin a tender in payment of debts, or passing any law impairing the obligation of contracts—supports his view that the "economic questions at issue between debtor and creditor" were not the basis for prolonged dispute or for compromise.

There is room to question, however, his statement that the economic questions at issue between "farmer and merchant" were not the subject of dispute and compromise. Disputes of this kind in the Convention were largely sectional in nature, and most of the disagreements and resulting compromises between the delegates from the southern states and those representing the northern states were more economic than political. These include such questions as the slave trade, the direct taxation of land and of slaves, the regulation of foreign commerce and the imposition of export duties. To use a classification which I employed some years ago in analyzing the political philosophy of the *Federalist,* the economic differences in the Convention reflected vertical rather than horizontal cleavages;[4] they were not between the bourgeoisie and the proletariat but rather between rival bourgeois, usually sectional, interests.

It is difficult to see the extent of the agreement in the Convention unless it is looked at in the light of comparative history. One must step outside of the Convention and consider not so much the day-to-day debates, as the principles and answers which they took for granted and rarely discussed.

Most significant of all the questions which might have been debated, but were not, was the principle of representative government. There was only one man in the Convention who spoke in favor of anything other than popular government as then understood, and that was Alexander Hamilton. But if Hamilton, in his speech of June 18, believed "that the British Government was the best in the world: and that he doubted much whether anything short of it would do in America," no other member of the Convention supported this plea for monarchy and hereditary privilege, nor did anyone propose holding elections other than at regular, fixed intervals. The system of ministerial responsibility and of elections following the loss of a majority in the Commons was imperfectly understood in England and either not understood or not approved in America. Moreover, from the beginning of the Convention, it seems to have been accepted by nearly all delegates present, even though some of the small state groups for a time apparently favored election by the state legislatures, that the lower House of the Federal Congress should be elected by popular vote. In the entire history of federal government there had never been a central legislative body elected by popular vote, certainly not in America where the Congress had been elected by the state legislatures. The small group seems not to have opposed popular election of the lower House, but rather to have supported equal voting power for the small states. After the Great Compromise no voice was raised against the principle of popular election. The delegates did not support popular election for the Senate or for the national executive or for the courts, but then it is to be remembered that nothing of this kind was found in the central government, that the upper houses in several states were elected by the lower, and that state judges were appointed by the governors or the legislatures.

The delegates unanimously assumed that there should be a written constitution with an amending clause. In the twentieth century virtually all countries follow that assumption; in the eighteenth century the Americans were almost unique among the nations in so doing.

The new government was then to be republican and it was to be based upon a written constitution which was fundamental law, one which could be changed by a special process. It was also to be far stronger, with many more effective powers, than the government under the Articles of Confederation. Even the New Jersey Plan extended the power to tax and to regulate commerce. It is evident that from the beginning of the debates, though there were disagreements over particulars, every member of the Convention agreed that the central government

---

[4] "The Federalist on the Nature of Political Man," *Ethics,* LIX, January 1949, no. 2, Part II, pp. 1–31.

should be more powerful. Some of the most important powers given to Congress by the Committee on Detail, which drafted the section enumerating the delegated powers, were accepted without debate. The principal differences of opinion, though not the only ones, were related to sectional issues.

It is of the greatest significance that the Convention accepted the principle that the central government should legislate for and tax individual persons. This, like the principle of popular election of the House and of representation in that body according to population, is a break with the history of federal government up to 1787. Before that time federal government had meant a league or confederation of sovereign or quasi-sovereign states, the central government having authority to deal with states but not with individual citizens. It should also be remembered, however, that the delegates did not agree with the principle of straight nationalism as Hamilton proposed. They accepted a mixed form, a new system combining nationalism and federalism. Since 1787 the term federal has come to mean a mixed system of this kind, the old kind of federalism usually being called a confederation.

Two of the most significant clauses, so far as the nature of this new or American federalism is concerned, are the supreme law clause and the necessary and proper clause which was inserted by the Committee on Detail. Neither of these clauses was the subject of debate.

Though there were numerous questions relating to the distribution of powers and to the relation of the Congress and the President, there was almost no dispute over the principle that the new government should be one in which there should be a separation of powers with its cor-

relative principle, checks and balances.[5] The point of view expressed by Roger Sherman early in the Convention was not debated, any more than was Hamilton's plan which would have vested a much larger share of power than was acceptable to the other delegates in the executive. This is one of the numerous subjects on which there was substantial and general agreement, though there were differences of opinion and frequent compromises on matters of detail.

Except for Franklin and one or two other delegates, unicameralism had no support in the Convention. To be sure the New Jersey Plan called for a unicameral legislature, but that was for the purpose of securing equality of voting power to the small states. When the Great Compromise was accepted, no more was heard of unicameralism. The delegates, with almost no exceptions, believed in bicameralism for the central government as they did for the states, and for the same reason, the distrust of unchecked power in any assembly, plus the need to give representation to the small states in the Senate. The statement sometimes made that the Senate is "a happy accident" is misleading. The principle that each state has the same number of representatives is the result of a compromise, though perhaps not the happiest of compromises or accidents, but bicameralism was the accepted principle from the beginning, as is made plain in the Virginia Plan and the early acceptance of that principle in it.

Similarly, from the beginning nearly all of the delegates agreed that there should be a single, rather than a plural, executive. Virtually all of the states had

---

[5] See my article cited above, "The Origins of the Separation of Powers in America," pp. 180–183.

single executives and almost all of the delegates, even most of those from Pennsylvania which had a plural executive, assumed and preferred a single President to anything corresponding to the British Ministry.

One of the major innovations was that the central government should have, not just one court of appeals, but a separate judicial system. That, like the popular election of the House and the authority of the central government to impose taxes and regulations directly upon individuals, was a new feature in a federal government. There was, however, greater difference of opinion over this point than over the other innovations just mentioned. After some debate, the Virginia proposal that Congress shall establish a system of lower courts was voted down by a vote of five states to three. When the motion was amended so that Congress could establish a system of lower courts, but was not required to do so, the proposal was accepted by the somewhat surprising majority of eight to two. Life tenure for the judges of the federal courts seems to have been assumed from the beginning.

Such were the agreements and disagreements of 1787. It is true, as Professor Schuyler and others have argued, that there were disputes and occasions for compromise over political questions. It is also true that the compromises were impressive. But far more impressive were the major assumptions upon which there was no need for compromise. The most fundamental political or constitutional issues were taken for granted without debate, or they were only briefly discussed. These include such basic issues as representative government, elections at fixed intervals, a written constitution which is a supreme law and which contains an amending clause, separation of powers and checks and balances, a bicameral legislature, a single executive, and a separate court system. These principles could have been taken for granted in no other country in the eighteenth century, nor could they in combination have been accepted in any other country even after discussion and vote. The nature and extent of this basic agreement throws far more light upon the political and constitutional thought of Americans in 1787 than do the disputes over questions which were nearly always matters of detail, or which were based largely upon sectional disagreement, or upon the size of the several states.

To put the matter another way: if Alexander Hamilton had had a dozen followers in the Convention, instead of none, or if Paine had been there and had had a group of sympathizers, there would have been far more disagreement over political and constitutional issues. Had both Hamilton and Paine been present and been supported by other delegates, the polarization of philosophies which would very likely have resulted might have made lasting agreement improbable, perhaps impossible. It is when we contrast the debates and the decisions of the Federal Convention with those of comparable bodies in many other countries that we see how great was the area of agreement and how essential it was to the lasting success of the Convention's work.

If this point of view seems exaggerated, I suggest that one recall the history of the struggle over such questions in other countries of modern times. In Philadelphia, monarchy, feudalism, and hereditary privilege were not issues. The delegates did not have to resolve the conflicting claims of church and state. Nor was there in this country such religious cleavage as made the union of all India impossible, when that subcontinent became independent a few years ago. There was no dispute even vaguely comparable to the struggles over capitalism versus communism which have torn countries apart and resulted in civil war and dictatorship during the last four decades. To the Americans of 1787 these fundamental questions were simply not issues.

My first purpose in this chapter has been to indicate the great and determining importance of agreement among the delegates. With a single exception, presently to be considered, virtually all of them held views which were identical, or so nearly so as to make for easy agreement on those basic subjects where lack of agreement has frequently made stable governments according to known and settled laws impossible.

A second, and not insignificant, aim has been to point out that the delegates were able, when they did disagree, to work out acceptable compromises or, more frequently, and just as essential, to accept defeat when outvoted. Had they been too proud, too stiff-necked, too intransigent, either to accept defeat when on the losing side, or unwilling to compromise their differences, the Convention would very likely have gone down in history as one of the many failures in the attempt to establish a workable and a lasting government. Fortunately for their posterity, the point of view which was accepted by most, though not by all of them, was that expressed feelingly by Benjamin Franklin on the last day of the Convention meetings, when the final draft, having been read, was before them for a vote. The aged Doctor urged that everyone who had remained to the last session sign the Constitution. He freely admitted that he did not agree with all of its provisions, but said that experience had taught him to doubt his own first judgments. More than once he had changed "opinions even on important subjects." He doubted whether another convention could "make a better constitution." It too would consist of men with prejudices, passions, local interests and errors of judgment, as well as wisdom. He asked that each of his colleagues who had objections to the Constitution "would with me, on this occasion doubt a little of his own infallibility, and . . . put his name to this instrument."*

Franklin's speech must have been the more impressive to the delegates who knew that he had been outvoted on a number of issues and that his point of view had, on others, been ignored.

Doubtless it is unecessary to labor the point that without agreement on certain fundamental questions a stable, constitutional government is impossible, and that without the willingness to accept a majority vote or, alternatively, to compromise differences, a government of laws will not long endure. The validity of these generalizations is supported by the results of the failure of the Convention to solve one great question, or pair of questions—slavery and the slave trade. No action was possible on the first, and the second was simply brushed under the rug, there to remain for twenty years.

Slavery existed in almost all of the states at that time. There was some antislavery sentiment, reflected in the Convention by Gouverneur Morris who said it is "a nefarious institution, . . . the curse of heaven on the States where it prevails," and by George Mason who spoke feelingly of the miserable effects of slavery on slave owners and poor alike and virtually prophesied "national calamities" if the institution should be continued and the slave area expanded. But the opposition to slavery at that time was not sufficiently general to permit either agreement or compromise on its abolition. Even that abominable traffic, the slave trade, could not be abolished. The southernmost states, to their later impoverishment and humiliation, threatened not to join the Union if power to prohibit the slave trade were given to Congress. On this point they were adamant.

The existence of slavery, its spread westward, the rise of burning opposition to it, together with the intransigence of the effective majority in the South and Southwest, eventually led to war. On that question, and only on that question, there was disagreement beyond the possibility either of submission to the vote of a majority, or of compromise. We have in that story the perfect, and tragic, example of the failure of constitutional methods. This failure serves to throw into clearer relief the extent to which there was a tremendous, and essential, area of agreement in the Convention, together with the ability either to compromise or to accept majority vote on issues where agreement was less than complete.

Ours has indeed been a fortunate, or a wise, and certainly a happier, country because the great issues which have divided us, have, with the single exception of slavery, been resolved without recourse to war. On most such issues the minority has accepted the decision of the majority. Others, many others, have been compromised.

I would not want to be understood as saying that all issues or principles can or should be compromised, or that the majority is always correct and the minority should always accept its decision. There are principles and issues which cannot be compromised; there are times when majority vote does not give a final answer. But history contains so many examples of an absolute conviction of self-rightness being founded on fanaticism and ignorance, of eternal principles which were no more than transitory policies, that the tolerant humility of Franklin seems the way of maturity and wisdom. If men could but agree on both aims and means, there would be few problems of politics to plague and divide us. So long as men remain prone to selfishness and emotion and fallible in judgment, a decent respect for the opinions of others and a willingness to compromise are essential to the continuance of constitutional government.

JOHN P. ROCHE (1923–   ) is Professor of Politics
at Brandeis University, Waltham, Massachusetts. In the
selection presented here, Roche views the drafting and
adoption of the Constitution as a case study in reform
politics. To him, the past political experience of the
members of the Philadelphia Convention was one of
their chief assets. This experience enabled them to
draft a document which fitted the needs of most
Americans so well that it could be accepted without a
great deal of opposition. To Roche, the Constitution
does not represent an exercise in political theory or
ideology but rather a moderately successful example
of the skill of the Founding Fathers as practical
politicians who made the most of their advantages.*

John P. Roche

Government-Making by Caucus

When the Constitutionalists went forth
to subvert the Confederation, they uti-
lized the mechanisms of political legitimacy. And the roadblocks which confronted them were formidable. At the
same time, they were endowed with certain potent political assets. The history
of the United States from 1786 to 1790
was largely one of a masterful employment of political expertise by the Constitutionalists as against bumbling, erratic
behavior by the opponents of reform.
Effectively, the Constitutionalists had to
induce the states, by democratic techniques of coercion, to emasculate themselves. To be specific, if New York had
refused to join the new Union, the project
was doomed; yet before New York was
safely in, the reluctant state legislature
had *sua sponte* to take the following steps:
(1) agree to send delegates to the Philadelphia Convention; (2) provide maintenance for these delegates (these were
distinct stages: New Hampshire was early
in naming delegates, but did not provide
for their maintenance until July); (3) set
up the special *ad hoc* convention to decide on ratification; and (4) concede to
the decision of the *ad hoc* convention that
New York should participate. New York
admittedly was a tricky state, with a strong
interest in a *status quo* which permitted
her to exploit New Jersey and Connecticut, but the same legal hurdles existed in every state. And at the risk of
becoming boring, it must be reiterated

*Reprinted by permission from John P. Roche, "The Founding Fathers: A Reform Caucus in Action,"
American Political Science Review, LV, No. 4 (December, 1961), 800–803, 812–816. Footnotes omitted.

that the *only* weapon in the Constitutionalist arsenal was an effective mobilization of public opinion.

The group which undertook this struggle was an interesting amalgam of a few dedicated nationalists with the self-interested spokesmen of various parochial bailiwicks. The Georgians, for example, wanted a strong central authority to provide military protection for their huge, underpopulated state against the Creek Confederacy; Jerseymen and Connecticuters wanted to escape from economic bondage to New York; the Virginians hoped to establish a system which would give that great state its rightful place in the councils of the republic. The dominant figures in the politics of these states therefore cooperated in the call for the Convention. In other states, the thrust towards national reform was taken up by opposition groups who added the "national interest" to their weapons system; in Pennsylvania, for instance, the group fighting to revise the Constitution of 1776 came out foursquare behind the Constitutionalists, and in New York, Hamilton and the Schuyler *ambiance* took the same tack against George Clinton. There was, of course, a large element of personality in the affair: there is reason to suspect that Patrick Henry's opposition to the Convention and the Constitution was founded on his conviction that Jefferson was behind both, and a close study of local politics elsewhere would surely reveal that others supported the Constitution for the simple (and politically quite sufficient) reason that the "wrong" people were against it.

To say this is not to suggest that the Constitution rested on a foundation of impure or base motives. It is rather to argue that in politics there are no immaculate conceptions, and that in the drive for a stronger general government, motives of all sorts played a part. Few men in the history of mankind have espoused a view of the "common good" or "public interest" that militated against their private status; even Plato with all his reverence for disembodied reason managed to put philosophers on top of the pile. Thus it is not surprising that a number of diversified private interests joined to push the nationalist public interest; what would have been surprising was the absence of such a pragmatic united front. And the fact remains that, however motivated, these men did demonstrate a willingness to compromise their parochial interests in behalf of an ideal which took shape before their eyes and under their ministrations.

As Stanley Elkins and Eric McKitrick have suggested in a perceptive essay, what distinguished the leaders of the Constitutionalist caucus from their enemies was a "Continental" approach to political, economic and military issues. To the extent that they shared an institutional base of operations, it was the Continental Congress (thirty-nine of the delegates to the Federal Convention had served in Congress), and this was hardly a locale which inspired respect for the state governments. Robert de Jouvenal observed French politics half a century ago and noted that a revolutionary Deputy had had more in common with a non-revolutionary Deputy than he had with a revolutionary non-Deputy; similarly one can surmise that membership in the Congress under the Articles of Confederation worked to establish a continental frame of reference, that a Congressman from Pennsylvania and one from North Carolina would share a universe of discourse which provided them with a conceptual common denominator *vis à vis* their respective state legislatures. This was particularly true with respect to external affairs: the average state legislator was probably about as concerned with foreign policy then as he is today, but Congressmen were constantly forced to take the broad view of American prestige, were compelled to listen to the reports of Secretary John Jay and to the dispatches and pleas from their frustrated envoys in Britain, France and Spain. From considerations such as these, a "Continental" ideology developed which seems to have demanded a revision of our domestic institutions primarily on the ground that only by invigorating our general government could we assume our rightful place in the international arena. Indeed, an argument with great force—particularly since Washington was its incarnation—urged that our very survival in the Hobbesian jungle of world politics depended upon a reordering and strengthening of our national sovereignty.

Note that I am not endorsing the "Critical Period" thesis; on the contrary, Merrill Jensen seems to me quite sound in his view that for most Americans, engaged as they were in self-sustaining agriculture, the "Critical Period" was not particularly critical. In fact, the great achievement of the Constitutionalists was their ultimate success in convincing the elected representatives of a majority of the white male population that change was imperative. A small group of political leaders with a Continental vision and essentially a consciousness of the United States' *international impotence*, provided the matrix of the movement. To their standard other leaders rallied with their own parallel ambitions. Their great assets were (1) the presence in their caucus of the one authentic American "father figure," George Washington, whose prestige was enormous; (2) the energy and talent of their leadership (in which

one must include the towering intellectuals of the time, John Adams and Thomas Jefferson, despite their absence abroad), and their communications "network," which was far superior to anything on the opposition side; (3) the preemptive skill which made "their" issue The Issue and kept the locally oriented opposition permanently on the defensive; and (4) the subjective consideration that these men were spokesmen of a new and compelling credo: *American* nationalism, that ill-defined but nonetheless potent sense of collective purpose that emerged from the American Revolution.

Despite great institutional handicaps, the Constitutionalists managed in the mid-1780s to mount an offensive which gained momentum as years went by. Their greatest problem was lethargy, and paradoxically, the number of barriers in their path may have proved an advantage in the long run. Beginning with the initial battle to get the Constitutional Convention called and delegates appointed, they could never relax, never let up the pressure. In practical terms, this meant that the local "organizations" created by the Constitutionalists were perpetually in movement building up their cadres for the next fight. (The word organization has to be used with great caution: a political organization in the United States—as in contemporary England—generally consisted of a magnate and his following, or a coalition of magnates. This did not necessarily mean that it was "undemocratic" or "aristocratic," in the Aristotelian sense of the word: while a few magnates such as the Livingstons could draft their followings, most exercised their leadership without coercion on the basis of popular endorsement. The absence of organized opposition did not imply the impossibility of competition any more than low public participation in elections necessarily indicated an undemocratic suffrage.)

The Constitutionalists got the jump on the "opposition" (a collective noun: oppositions would be more correct) at the outset with the demand for a Convention. Their opponents were caught in an old political trap: they were not being asked to approve any specific program of reform, but only to endorse a meeting to discuss and recommend needed reforms. If they took a hard line at the first stage, they were put in the position of glorifying the *status quo* and of denying the need for *any* changes. Moreover, the Constitutionalists could go to the people with a persuasive argument for "fair play"—"How can you condemn reform before you know precisely what is involved?" Since the state legislatures obviously would have the final say on any proposals that might emerge from the Convention, the Constitutionalists were merely reasonable men asking for a chance. Besides, since they did not make any concrete proposals at that stage, they were in a position to capitalize on every sort of generalized discontent with the Confederation.

Perhaps because of their poor intelligence system, perhaps because of overconfidence generated by the failure of all previous efforts to alter the Articles, the opposition awoke too late to the dangers that confronted them in 1787. Not only did the Constitutionalists manage to get every state but Rhode Island (where politics was enlivened by a party system reminiscent of the "Blues" and the "Greens" in the Byzantine Empire) to appoint delegates to Philadelphia, but when the results were in, it appeared that they dominated the delegations. Given the apathy of the opposition, this was a natural phenomenon: in an ideologically nonpolarized political atmosphere those who get appointed to

a special committee are likely to be the men who supported the movement for its creation. Even George Clinton, who seems to have been the first opposition leader to awake to the possibility of trouble, could not prevent the New York legislature from appointing Alexander Hamilton—though he did have the foresight to send two of his henchmen to dominate the delegation. Incidentally, much has been made of the fact that the delegates to Philadelphia were not elected by the people; some have adduced this fact as evidence of the "undemocratic" character of the gathering. But put in the context of the time, this argument is wholly specious: the central government under the Articles was considered a creature of the component states and in all the states but Rhode Island, Connecticut and New Hampshire, members of the national Congress were chosen by the state legislatures. This was not a consequence of elitism or fear of the mob; it was a logical extension of states'-rights doctrine to guarantee that the national institution did not end-run the state legislatures and make direct contact with the people.

Drawing on their vast collective political experience, utilizing every weapon in the politician's arsenal, looking constantly over their shoulders at their constituents, the delegates put together a Constitution. It was a makeshift affair; some sticky issues (for example, the qualification of voters) they ducked entirely; others they mastered with that ancient instrument of political sagacity, studied ambiguity (for example, citizenship), and some they just overlooked. In this last category, I suspect, fell the matter of the power of the federal courts to determine the constitutionality of acts of Congress. When the judicial article was formulated (Article III of the Constitution), deliberations were still in the stage where the legislature was endowed with broad power under the Randolph formulation, authority which by its own terms was scarcely amenable to judicial review. In essence, courts could hardly determine when " . . . the separate States are incompetent or . . . the harmony of the United States may be interrupted"; the National Legislature, as critics pointed out, was free to define its own jurisdiction. Later the definition of legislative authority was changed into the form we know, a series of stipulated powers, *but the delegates never seriously reexamined the jurisdiction of the judiciary under this new limited formulation.* All arguments on the intention of the Framers in this matter are thus deductive and *a posteriori,* though some obviously make more sense than others.

The Framers were busy and distinguished men, anxious to get back to their families, their positions, and their constituents, not members of the French Academy devoting a lifetime to a dictionary. They were trying to do an important job, and do it in such a fashion that their handwork would be acceptable to very diverse constituencies. No one was rhapsodic about the final document, but it was a beginning, a move in the right direction, and one they had reason to believe the people would endorse. In addition, since they had modified the impossible amendment provisions of the Articles (the requirement of unanimity which could always be frustrated by "Rogues Island") to one demanding approval by only three-quarters of the states, they seemed confident that gaps in the fabric which experience would reveal could be rewoven without undue difficulty.

So with a neat phrase introduced by

Benjamin Franklin (but devised by Gouverneur Morris) which made their decision sound unanimous, and an inspired benediction by the Old Doctor urging doubters to doubt their own infallibility, the Constitution was accepted and signed. Curiously, Edmund Randolph, who had played so vital a role throughout, refused to sign, as did his fellow Virginian George Mason and Elbridge Gerry of Massachusetts. Randolph's behavior was eccentric, to say the least—his excuses for refusing his signature have a factitious ring even at this late date; the best explanation seems to be that he was afraid that the Constitution would prove to be a liability in Virginia politics, where Patrick Henry was burning up the countryside with impassioned denunciations. Presumably, Randolph wanted to check the temper of the populace before he risked his reputation, and perhaps his job, in a fight with both Henry and Richard Henry Lee. Events lend some justification to this speculation: after much temporizing and use of the conditional subjunctive tense, Randolph endorsed ratification in Virginia and ended up getting the best of both worlds.

Madison, despite his reservations about the Constitution, was the campaign manager in ratification. His first task was to get the Congress in New York to light its own funeral pyre by approving the "amendments" to the Articles and sending them on to the state legislatures. Above all, momentum had to be maintained. The anti-Constitutionalists, now thoroughly alarmed and no novices in politics, realized that their best tactic was attrition rather than direct opposition. Thus they settled on a position expressing qualified approval but calling for a second Convention to remedy various defects (the one with the most demagogic appeal was the lack of a Bill of Rights). Madison knew that to accede to this demand would be equivalent to losing the battle, nor would he agree to conditional approval (despite wavering even by Hamilton). This was an all-or-nothing proposition: national salvation or national impotence with no intermediate positions possible. Unable to get congressional approval, he settled for second best: a unanimous resolution of Congress transmitting the Constitution to the states for whatever action they saw fit to take. The opponents then moved from New York and the Congress, where they had attempted to attach amendments and conditions, to the states for the final battle.

At first the campaign for ratification went beautifully: within eight months after the delegates set their names on the document, eight states had ratified. Only in Massachusetts had the result been close (187–168). Theoretically, a ratification by one more state convention would set the new government in motion, but in fact until Virginia and New York acceded to the new Union, the latter was fiction. New Hampshire was the next to ratify; Rhode Island was involved in its characteristic political convulsions (the Legislature there sent the Constitution out to the towns for decision by popular vote and it got lost among a series of local issues); North Carolina's convention did not meet until July and then postponed a final decision. This is hardly the place for an extensive analysis of the conventions of New York and Virginia. Suffice it to say that the Constitutionalists clearly outmaneuvered their opponents, forced them into impossible political positions, and won both states narrowly. The Virginia Convention could serve as a classic study in effective floor management: Patrick Henry had to be contained, and a reading of the debates discloses

a standard two-stage technique. Henry would give a four-or-five-hour speech denouncing some section of the Constitution on every conceivable ground (the federal district, he averred at one point, would become a haven for convicts escaping from state authority!); when Henry subsided, "Mr. Lee of Westmoreland" would rise and literally poleaxe him with sardonic invective (when Henry complained about the militia power, "Lighthorse Harry" really punched below the belt: observing that while the former Governor had been sitting in Richmond during the Revolution, *he* had been out in the trenches with the troops and thus felt better qualified to discuss military affairs). Then the gentlemanly Constitutionalists (Madison, Pendleton and Marshall) would pick up the matters at issue and examine them in the light of reason.

Indeed, modern Americans who tend to think of James Madison as a rather desiccated character should spend some time with this transcript. Probably Madison put on his most spectacular demonstration of nimble rhetoric in what might be called "The Battle of the Absent Authorities." Patrick Henry in the course of one of his harangues alleged that Jefferson was known to be opposed to Virginia's approving the Constitution. This was clever: Henry hated Jefferson, but was prepared to use any weapon that came to hand. Madison's riposte was superb: First, he said that with all due respect to the great reputation of Jefferson, he was not in the country and therefore could not formulate an adequate judgment; second, no one should utilize the reputation of an outsider—the Virginia Convention was there to think for itself; third, if there were to be recourse to outsiders, the opinions of George Washington should certainly be taken into consideration; and finally, he knew from privileged personal communication from Jefferson that in fact the latter *strongly favored* the Constitution. To devise an assault route into this rhetorical fortress was literally impossible.

The fight was over; all that remained now was to establish the new frame of government in the spirit of its framers. And who were better qualified for this task than the Framers themselves? Thus victory for the Constitution meant simultaneous victory for the Constitutionalists; the anti-Constitutionalists either capitulated or vanished into limbo—soon Patrick Henry would be offered a seat on the Supreme Court and Luther Martin would be known as the Federalist "bull-dog." And irony of ironies, Alexander Hamilton and James Madison would shortly accumulate a reputation as the formulators of what is often alleged to be our political theory, the concept of "federalism." Also, on the other side of the ledger, the arguments would soon appear over what the Framers "really meant"; while these disputes have assumed the proportions of a big scholarly business in the last century, they began almost before the ink on the Constitution was dry. One of the best early ones featured Hamilton versus Madison on the scope of presidential power, and other Framers characteristically assumed positions in this and other disputes on the basis of their political convictions.

Probably our greatest difficulty is that we know so much more about what the Framers *should have meant* than they themselves did. We are intimately acquainted with the problems that their Constitution should have been designed to master; in short, we have read the mystery story backwards. If we are to get the right "feel" for their time and their circumstances, we must in Maitland's phrase, " . . . think ourselves back into the twilight." Obviously, no one can pretend completely to escape from the solipsistic web of his own environment, but if the effort is made, it is possible to appreciate the past roughly on its own terms. The first step in this process is to abandon the academic premise that because we can ask a question, there must be an answer.

Thus we can ask what the Framers meant when they gave Congress the power to regulate interstate and foreign commerce, and we emerge, reluctantly perhaps, with the reply that . . . they may not have known what they meant, that there may not have been any semantic consensus. The Convention was not a seminar in analytic philosophy or linguistic analysis. Commerce was *commerce* and if different interpretations of the word arose, later generations could worry about the problem of definition. The delegates were in a hurry to get a new government established; when definitional arguments arose, they characteristically took refuge in ambiguity. If different men voted for the same proposition for varying reasons, that was politics (and still is); if later generations were unsettled by this lack of precision, that would be their problem.

There was a good deal of definitional pluralism with respect to the problems the delegates did discuss, but when we move to the question of extrapolated intentions, we enter the realm of spiritualism. When men in our time, for instance, launch into elaborate talmudic exegesis to demonstrate that federal aid to parochial schools is (or is not) in accord with the intentions of the men who established the Republic and endorsed the Bill of Rights, they are engaging in historical Extra-Sensory Perception. (If one were to join this E.S.P. contingent for a minute, he might suggest that the hard-boiled politicians who wrote the Constitution and Bill of Rights would chuckle scornfully at such an invocation of authority: obviously a politician would chart his course on the intentions of the living, not of the dead, and count the numbers of Catholics in his constituency.)

The Constitution, then, was not an apotheosis of "constitutionalism," a triumph of architectonic genius; it was a patch-work sewn together under the pressure of both time and events by a group of extremely talented democratic politicians. They refused to attempt the establishment of a strong, centralized sovereignty on the principle of legislative supremacy for the excellent reason that the people would not accept it. They risked their political fortunes by opposing the established doctrines of state sovereignty because they were convinced that the existing system was leading to national impotence and probably foreign domination. For two years, they worked to get a convention established. For over three months, in what must have seemed to the faithful participants an endless process of give-and-take, they reasoned, cajoled, threatened, and bargained amongst themselves. The result was a Constitution which the people, in fact, by democratic processes, did accept, and a new and far better national government was established.

Beginning with the inspired propaganda of Hamilton, Madison and Jay, the ideological build-up got under way. *The Federalist* had little impact on the ratification of the Constitution, except perhaps in New York, but his volume had enormous influence on the image of the Constitution in the minds of future genera-

tions, particularly on historians and political scientists who have an innate fondness for theoretical symmetry. Yet, while the shades of Locke and Montesquieu *may* have been hovering in the background, and the delegates *may* have been unconscious instruments of a transcendent *telos,* the careful observer of the day-to-day work of the Convention finds no over-arching principles. The "separation of powers" to him seems to be a by-product of suspicion, and "federalism" he views as a *pis aller,* as the farthest point the delegates felt they could go in the destruction of state power without themselves inviting repudiation.

To conclude, the Constitution was neither a victory for abstract theory nor a great practical success. Well over half a million men had to die on the battlefields of the Civil War before certain constitutional principles could be defined—a baleful consideration which is somehow overlooked in our customary tributes to the farsighted genius of the Framers and to the supposed American talent for "constitutionalism." The Constitution was, however, a vivid demonstration of effective democratic political action, and of the forging of a national elite which literally persuaded its countrymen to hoist themselves by their own boot straps. American pro-consuls would be wise not to translate the Constitution into Japanese, or Swahili, or treat it as a work of semi-Divine origin; but when students of comparative politics examine the process of nation-building in countries newly freed from colonial rule they may find the American experience instructive as a classic example of the potentialities of a democratic elite.

GORDON WOOD (1933–   ) is Professor of History at Brown University. In this excerpt from his book *The Creation of the American Republic, 1776–1787,* Wood views the Federalist-Antifederalist argument as a far-reaching disagreement over the nature of political society. Opposed to the Federalist conception of an organic society led politically by a natural aristocracy, the Antifederalists saw society as made up of distinct interests and classes, all of which had to be represented in government. The challenge thrown up by the Antifederalists to the Constitution showed how fragile the aristocratic republic of the Federalists was. Implicit in Wood's argument is Beard's assumption that the Federalists were conservative republicans and the Antifederalists were radical democrats. To what extent has this assumption been supported or undermined by the previous articles?*

Gordon Wood

Worthy Aristocrats versus Licentious Democrats

The division over the Constitution in 1787–88 is not easily analyzed. It is difficult, as historians have recently demonstrated, to equate the supporters or opponents of the Constitution with particular economic groupings. The Antifederalist politicians in the ratifying conventions often possessed wealth, including public securities, equal to that of the Federalists. While the relative youth of the Federalist leaders, compared to the ages of the prominent Antifederalists, was important, especially in accounting for the Federalists' ability to think freshly and creatively about politics, it can hardly be used to explain the division throughout the country. Moreover, the

concern of the 1780s with America's moral character was not confined to the proponents of the Constitution. That rabid republican and Antifederalist, Benjamin Austin, was as convinced as any Federalist that "the luxurious living of all ranks and degrees" was "the principal cause of all the evils we now experience." Some leading Antifederalist intellectuals expressed as much fear of "the injustice, folly, and wickedness of the State Legislatures" and of "the usurpation and tyranny of the majority" against the minority as did Madison. In the Philadelphia Convention both Mason and Elbridge Gerry, later prominent Antifederalists, admitted "the danger of the levelling spirit" flow-

*Reprinted by permission from Gordon Wood, *The Creation of the American Republic, 1776–1787* (Chapel Hill: University of North Carolina Press for the Institute of Early American History and Culture, 1969), pp. 483–499. Footnotes omitted.

ing from "the excess of democracy" in the American republics. There were many diverse reasons in each state why men supported or opposed the Constitution that cut through any sort of class division. The Constitution was a single issue in a complicated situation, and its acceptance or rejection in many states was often dictated by peculiar circumstances—the prevalence of Indians, the desire for western lands, the special interests of commerce—that defy generalization. Nevertheless, despite all of this confusion and complexity, the struggle over the Constitution, as the debate if nothing else makes clear, can best be understood as a social one. Whatever the particular constituency of the antagonists may have been, men in 1787–88 talked as if they were representing distinct and opposing social elements. Both the proponents and opponents of the Constitution focused throughout the debates on an essential point of political sociology that ultimately must be used to distinguish a Federalist from an Antifederalist. The quarrel was fundamentally one between aristocracy and democracy.

Because of its essentially social base, this quarrel, as George Minot of Massachusetts said, was "extremely unequal." To be sure, many Antifederalists, especially in Virginia, were as socially and intellectually formidable as any Federalist. Richard Henry Lee was undoubtedly the strongest mind the Antifederalists possessed, and he sympathized with the Antifederalist cause. Like Austin and other Antifederalists he believed that moral regeneration of America's character, rather than any legalistic manipulation of the constitutions of government, was the proper remedy for America's problems. "I fear," he wrote to George Mason in May 1787, "it is more in vicious manners, than mistakes in form, that we

must seek for the causes of the present discontent." Still, such "aristocrats" as Lee or Mason did not truly represent Antifederalism. Not only did they reject the vicious state politics of the 1780s which Antifederalism, by the very purpose of the Constitution, was implicitly if not always explicitly committed to defend, but they could have no real identity, try as they might, with those for whom they sought to speak. Because, as Lee pointed out, "we must recollect how disproportionately the democratic and aristocratic parts of the community were represented" not only in the Philadelphia Convention but also in the ratifying conventions, many of the real Antifederalists, those intimately involved in the democratic politics of the 1780s and consequently with an emotional as well as an intellectual commitment to Antifederalism, were never clearly heard in the formal debates of 1787–88.

The disorganization and inertia of the Antifederalists, especially in contrast with the energy and effectiveness of the Federalists, has been repeatedly emphasized. The opponents of the Constitution lacked both coordination and unified leadership; "their principles," wrote Oliver Ellsworth, "are totally opposite to each other, and their objections discordant and irreconcilable." The Federalist victory, it appears, was actually more of an Antifederalist default. "We had no principle of concert or union," lamented the South Carolina Antifederalist, Aedanus Burke, while the supporters of the Constitution "left no expedient untried to push it forward." Madison's description of the Massachusetts Antifederalists was applicable to nearly all the states: "There was not a single character capable of uniting their wills or directing their measures. . . . They had no plan whatever. They looked no farther than to put a negative on the Constitution and return home." They were not, as one Federalist put it, "good politicians."

But the Antifederalists were not simply poorer politicians than the Federalists; they were actually different kinds of politicians. Too many of them were state-centered men with local interests and loyalties only, politicians without influence and connections, and ultimately politicians without social and intellectual confidence. In South Carolina the up-country opponents of the Constitution shied from debate and when they did occasionally rise to speak apologized effusively for their inability to say what they felt had to be said, thus leaving most of the opposition to the Constitution to be voiced by Rawlins Lowndes, a low-country planter who scarcely represented their interests and soon retired from the struggle. Elsewhere, in New Hampshire, Connecticut, Massachusetts, Pennsylvania, and North Carolina, the situation was similar: the Federalists had the bulk of talent and influence on their side "together with all the Speakers in the State great and small." In convention after convention the Antifederalists, as in Connecticut, tried to speak, but "they were browbeaten by many of those Cicero'es as they think themselves and others of Superior rank." "The presses are in a great measure secured to *their* side," the Antifederalists complained with justice: out of a hundred or more newspapers printed in the late eighties only a dozen supported the Antifederalists, as editors, "afraid to offend the great men, or Merchants, who could work their ruin," closed their columns to the opposition. The Antifederalists were not so much beaten as overawed. In Massachusetts the two leading socially established Antifederalists, Elbridge Gerry and James Warren, were defeated as delegates to

the Ratifying Convention, and Antifederalist leadership consequently fell into the hands of newer, self-made men, of whom Samuel Nasson was perhaps typical —a Maine shopkeeper who was accused of delivering ghostwritten speeches in the Convention. Nasson had previously sat in the General Court but had declined reelection because he had been too keenly made aware of "the want of a proper Education I feel my Self So Small on many occasions that I all most Scrink into Nothing Besides I am often obliged to Borrow from Gentlemen that had advantages which I have not." Now, however, he had become the stoutest of Antifederalists, "full charged with Gass," one of those grumblers who, as Rufus King told Madison, were more afraid of the proponents of the Constitution than the Constitution itself, frightened that "some injury is plotted against them" because of "the extraordinary Union in favor of the Constitution in this State of the Wealthy and sensible part of it."

This fear of a plot by men who "talk so finely and gloss over matters so smoothly" ran through the Antifederalist mind. Because the many "new men" of the 1780s, men like Melancthon Smith and Abraham Yates of New York or John Smilie and William Findley of Pennsylvania, had bypassed the social hierarchy in their rise to political leadership, they lacked those attributes of social distinction and dignity that went beyond mere wealth. Since these kinds of men were never assimilated to the gentlemanly cast of the Livingstons or the Morrises, they, like Americans earlier in confrontation with the British court, tended to view with suspicion and hostility the high-flying world of style and connections that they were barred by their language and tastes, if by nothing else, from sharing in. In the minds of these

socially inferior politicians the movement for the strengthening of the central
government could only be a "conspiracy"
"planned and set to work" by a few aristocrats, who were at first, said Abraham
Yates, no larger in number in any one
state than the cabal which sought to undermine English liberty at the beginning
of the eighteenth century. Since men like
Yates could not quite comprehend what
they were sure were the inner maneuver-
ings of the elite, they were convinced that
in the aristocrats' program, "what was
their view in the beginning" or how "far
it was Intended to be carried Must be
Collected from facts that Afterwards have
happened." Like American Whigs in the
sixties and seventies forced to delve into
the dark and complicated workings of
English court politics, they could judge
motives and plans "but by the Event."
And they could only conclude that the
events of the eighties, "the treasury, the
Cincinnati, and other public creditors,
with all their concomitants," were "somehow or other, . . . inseparably connected,"
were all parts of a grand design "con-
certed by a few *tyrants*" to undo the
Revolution and to establish an aristocracy
in order "to lord it over the rest of their
fellow citizens, to trample the poorer
part of the people under their feet, that
they may be rendered their servants and
slaves." In this climate all the major issues
of the Confederation period—the impost,
commutation, and the return of the Loyalists—possessed a political and social significance that transcended economic
concerns. All seemed to be devices by
which a ruling few, like the ministers of
the English Crown, would attach a corps
of pensioners and dependents to the government and spread their influence and
connections throughout the states in order
"to dissolve our present Happy and
Benevolent Constitution and to erect on
the Ruins, a proper Aristocracy."

Nothing was more characteristic of
Antifederalist thinking than this obses-
sion with aristocracy. Although to a
European, American society may have
appeared remarkably egalitarian, to
many Americans, especially to those
who aspired to places of consequence but
were made to feel their inferiority in
innumerable, often subtle, ways, American society was distinguished by its inequality. "It is true," said Melancton
Smith in the New York Ratifying Convention, "it is our singular felicity that
we have no legal or hereditary distinctions . . . ; but still there are real
differences." "Every society naturally
divides itself into classes. . . . Birth,
education, talents, and wealth, create
distinctions among men as visible, and of
as much influence, as titles, stars, and
garters." Everyone knew those "whom
nature hath destined to rule," declared
one sardonic Antifederalist pamphlet.
Their "qualifications of authority" were
obvious: "such as the dictatorial air, the
magisterial voice, the imperious tone,
the haughty countenance, the lofty look,
the majestic mien." In all communities,
"even in those of the most democratic
kind," wrote George Clinton (whose
"family and connections" in the minds
of those like Philip Schuyler did not
"entitle him to so distinguished a predominance" as the governorship of New
York), there were pressures—"superior
talents, fortunes and public employ-
ments"—demarcating an aristocracy
whose influence was difficult to resist.

Such influence was difficult to resist
because, to the continual annoyance of
the Antifederalists, the great body of the
people willingly submitted to it. The
"authority of names" and "the influence
of the great" among ordinary people
were too evident to be denied. "Will any
one say that there does not exist in this
country the pride of family, of wealth, of

talents, and that they do not command influence and respect among the common people?" "The people are too apt to yield an implicit assent to the opinions of those characters whose abilities are held in the highest esteem, and to those in whose integrity and patriotism they can confide; not considering that the love of domination is generally in proportion to talents, abilities and superior requirements." Because of this habit of deference in the people, it was "in the power of the enlightened and aspiring few, if they should combine, at any time to destroy the best establishments, and even make the people the instruments of their own subjugation." Hence, the Antifederalist-minded declared, the people must be awakened to the consequences of their self-ensnarement; they must be warned over and over by popular tribunes, by "those who are competent to the task of developing the principles of government," of the dangers involved in paying obeisance to those who they thought were their superiors. The people must "not be permitted to consider themselves as a grovelling, distinct species, uninterested in the general welfare."

Such constant admonitions to the people of the perils flowing from their too easy deference to the *"natural aristocracy"* were necessary because the Antifederalists were convinced that these "men that had been delicately bred, and who were in affluent circumstances," these "men of the most exalted rank in life," were by their very conspicuousness irreparably cut off from the great body of the people and hence could never share in its concerns nor look after its interests. It was not that these "certain men exalted above the rest" were necessarily "destitute of morality or virtue" or that they were inherently different from other men. "The same passions and prejudices govern all men." It was only that cir-

cumstances in their particular environment had made them different. There was "a charm in politicks"; men in high office become habituated with power, "grow fond of it, and are loath to resign it"; "they feel themselves flattered and elevated," enthralled by the attractions of high living, and thus they easily forget the interests of the common people, from which many of them once sprang. By dwelling so vividly on the allurements of prestige and power, by emphasizing again and again how the "human soul is affected by wealth, in all its faculties, . . . by its present interest, by its expectations, and by its fears," these ambitious Antifederalist politicians may have revealed as much about themselves as they did about the "aristocratic" elite they sought to displace. Yet at the same time by such language they contributed to a new appreciation of the nature of society.

In these repeated attacks on deference and the capacity of a conspicuous few to speak for the whole society—which was to become in time the distinguishing feature of American democratic politics— the Antifederalists struck at the roots of the traditional conception of political society. If the natural elite, whether its distinctions were ascribed or acquired, was not in any organic way connected to the "feelings, circumstances, and interests" of the people and was incapable of feeling "sympathetically the wants of the people," then it followed that only ordinary men, men not distinguished by the characteristics of aristocratic wealth and taste, men "in middling circumstances" untempted by the attractions of a cosmopolitan world and thus "more temperate, of better morals, and less ambitious, than the great," could be trusted to speak for the great body of the people, for those who were coming more and more to be referred to as "the middling and lower classes of people." The differentiating influence of the environment was such that men in various ranks and classes now seemed to be broken apart from one another, separated by their peculiar circumstances into distinct, unconnected, and often incompatible interests. With their indictment of aristocracy the Antifederalists were saying, whether they realized it or not, that the people of America even in their several states were not homogeneous entities each with a basic similarity of interest for which an empatic elite could speak. Society was not an organic hierarchy composed of ranks and degrees indissolubly linked one to another; rather it was a heterogeneous mixture of "many different classes or orders of people, Merchants, Farmers, Planter Mechanics and Gentry or wealthy Men." In such a society men from one class or group, however educated and respectable they may have been, could never be acquainted with the "*Situation* and Wants" of those of another class or group. Lawyers and planters could never be "adequate judges of tradesmens concerns." If men were truly to represent the people in government, it was not enough for them to be for the people; they had to be actually of the people. "Farmers, traders and mechanics . . . all ought to have a competent number of their best informed members in the legislature."

Thus the Antifederalists were not only directly challenging the conventional belief that only a gentlemanly few, even though now in America naturally and not artificially qualified, were best equipped through learning and experience to represent and to govern the society, but they were as well indirectly denying the assumption of organic social homogeneity on which republicanism rested. Without fully comprehending the consequences of their arguments the Antifederalists

were destroying the great chain of being, thus undermining the social basis of republicanism and shattering that unity and harmony of social and political authority which the eighteenth century generally and indeed most Revolutionary leaders had considered essential to the maintenance of order.

Confronted with such a fundamental challenge the Federalists initially backed away. They had no desire to argue the merits of the Constitution in terms of its social implications and were understandably reluctant to open up the character of American society as the central issue of the debate. But in the end they could not resist defending those beliefs in elitism that lay at the heart of their conception of politics and of their constitutional program. All of the Federalists' desires to establish a strong and respectable nation in the world, all of their plans to create a flourishing commercial economy, in short, all of what the Federalists wanted out of the new central government seemed in the final analysis dependent upon the prerequisite maintenance of aristocratic politics.

At first the Federalists tried to belittle the talk of an aristocracy; they even denied that they knew the meaning of the word. "Why bring into the debate the whims of writers—introducing the distinction of *well-born* from others?" asked Edmund Pendleton in the Virginia Ratifying Convention. In the Federalist view every man was "*well-born* who comes into the world with an intelligent mind, and with all his parts perfect." Was even natural talent to be suspect? Was learning to be encouraged, the Federalists asked in exasperation, only "to set up those who attained its benefits as butts of invidious distinction?" No American, the Federalists said, could justifiably oppose a man "commencing in life without any other stock but industry and economy," and "by the mere efforts of these" rising "to opulence and wealth." If social mobility were to be meaningful then some sorts of distinctions were necessary. If government by a natural aristocracy, said Wilson, meant "nothing more or less than a government of the best men in the community," then who could object to it? Could the Antifederalists actually intend to mark out those "most noted for their virtue and talents . . . as the most improper persons for the public confidence?" No, the Federalists exclaimed in disbelief, the Antifederalists could never have intended such a socially destructive conclusion. It was clear, said Hamilton, that the Antifederalists' arguments only proved "that there are men who are rich, men who are poor, some who are wise, and others who are not; that indeed, every distinguished man is an aristocrat."

But the Antifederalist intention and implication were too conspicuous to be avoided: all distinctions, whether naturally based or not, were being challenged. Robert Livingston in the New York Convention saw as clearly as anyone what he thought the Antifederalists were really after, and he minced no words in replying to Smith's attack on the natural aristocracy. Since Smith had classified as aristocrats not only "the rich and the great" but also "the wise, the learned, and those eminent for their talents or great virtues," aristocrats to the Antifederalists had in substance become all men of merit. Such men, such aristocrats, were not to be chosen for public office, questioned Livingston in rising disbelief in the implications of the Antifederalist argument, "because the people will not have confidence in them; that is, the people will not have confidence in those who best deserve and most

possess their confidence?" The logic of Smith's reasoning, said Livingston, would lead to a government by the dregs of society, a monstrous government where all "the unjust, the selfish, the unsocial feelings," where all "the vices, the infirmities, the passions of the people" would be represented. "Can it be thought," asked Livingston in an earlier development of this argument to the Society of the Cincinnati, "that an enlightened people believe the science of government level to the meanest capacity? That experience, application, and education are unnecessary to those who are to frame laws for the government of the state?" Yet strange as it may have seemed to Livingston and others in the 1780s, America was actually approaching the point where ability, education, and wealth were becoming liabilities, not assets, in the attaining of public office. "Envy and the ambition of the unworthy" were robbing respectable men of the rank they merited. "To these causes," said Livingston, "we owe the cloud that obscures our internal governments."

The course of the debates over the Constitution seemed to confirm what the Federalists had believed all along. Antifederalism represented the climax of a "war" that was, in the words of Theodore Sedgwick, being "levied on the virtue, property, and distinctions in the community." The opponents of the Constitution, despite some, "particularly in Virginia," who were operating "from the most honorable and patriotic motives," were essentially identical with those who were responsible for the evils the states were suffering from in the eighties — "narrowminded politicians . . . under the influence of local views." "Whilst many *ostensible* reasons are assigned" for the Antifederalists' opposition, charged Washington, "the real ones are concealed behind the Curtains, because they are not of a nature to appear in open day." "The real object of all their zeal in opposing the system," agreed Madison, was to maintain "the supremacy of the State Legislatures," with all that meant in the printing of money and the violation of contracts. The Antifederalists or those for whom the Antifederalists spoke, whether their spokesmen realized it or not, were "none but the horse-jockey, the mushroom merchant, the running and dishonest speculator," those "who owe the most and have the least to pay," those "whose dependence and expectations are upon changes in government, and distracted times," men of "desperate Circumstances," those "in Every State" who "have Debts to pay, Interests to support or Fortunes to make," those, in short, who "wish for scrambling Times." Apart from a few of their intellectual leaders the Antifederalists were thought to be an ill-bred lot: "Their education has been rather indifferent—they have been accustomed to think on the small scale." They were often blustering demagogues trying to push their way into office—"men of much self-importance and supposed skill in politics, who are not of sufficient consequence to obtain public employment." Hence they were considered to be jealous and mistrustful of "every one in the higher offices of society," unable to bear to see others possessing "that fancied blessing, to which, alas! they must themselves aspire in vain." In the Federalist mind therefore the struggle over the Constitution was not one between kinds of wealth or property, or one between commercial or noncommercial elements of the population, but rather represented a broad social division between those who believed in the right of a natural aristocracy to speak for the people and those who did not.

Against this threat from the licentious the Federalists pictured themselves as the defenders of the worthy, of those whom they called "the better sort of people," those, said John Jay, "who are orderly and industrious, who are content with their situations and not uneasy in their circumstances." Because the Federalists were fearful that republican equality was becoming "that *perfect equality* which deadens the motives of industry, and places Demerit on a Footing with Virtue," they were obsessed with the need to insure that the proper amount of inequality and natural distinctions be recognized. "Although there are no nobles in America," observed the French minister to America, Louis Otto, in 1786, "there is a class of men denominated 'gentlemen,' who, by reason of their wealth, their talents, their education, their families, or the offices they hold, aspire to a preeminence which the people refuse to grant them." "How idle . . . all disputes about a technical aristocracy" would be, if only the people would "pay strict attention to the natural aristocracy, which is the institution of heaven. . . . This aristocracy is derived from merit and that influence, which a character for superiour wisdom, and known services to the commonwealth, has to produce veneration, confidence and esteem, among a people, who have felt the benefits. . . . " Robert Morris, for example, was convinced there were social differences—even in Pennsylvania. "What!" he exclaimed in scornful amazement at John Smilie's argument that a republic admitted of no social superiorities. "Is it insisted that there is no distinction of character?" Respectability, said Morris with conviction, was not confined to property. "Surely persons possessed of knowledge, judgment, information, integrity, and having extensive connections, are not to be classed with persons void of reputation or character."

In refuting the Antifederalists' contention "that all classes of citizens should have some of their own number in the representative body, in order that their feelings and interests may be the better understood and attended to," Hamilton in *The Federalist,* Number 35, put into words the Federalists' often unspoken and vaguely held assumption about the organic and the hierarchical nature of society. Such explicit class or occupational representation as the Antifederalists advocated, wrote Hamilton, was not only impractical but unnecessary, since the society was not as fragmented or heterogeneous as the Antifederalists implied. The various groups in the landed interest, for example, were "perfectly united, from the wealthiest landlord down to the poorest tenant," and this "common interest may always be reckoned upon as the surest bond of sympathy" linking the landed representative, however rich, to his constituents. In a like way, the members of the commercial community were "immediately connected" and most naturally represented by the merchants. "Mechanics and manufacturers will always be inclined, with few exceptions, to give their votes to merchants, in preference to persons of their own professions or trades. . . . They know that the merchant is their natural patron and friend; and . . . they are sensible that their habits in life have not been such as to give them those acquired endowments, without which in a deliberative assembly, the greatest natural abilities, are for the most part useless." However much many Federalists may have doubted the substance of Hamilton's analysis of American society, they could not doubt the truth of his conclusion. That the people were represented better by one of the natural aristocracy "whose situation leads to extensive inquiry and information" than by one "whose observation does not travel beyond the circle of his neighbors and acquaintances" was the defining element of the Federalist philosophy.

It was not simply the number of public securities, or credit outstanding, or the number of ships, or the amount of money possessed that made a man think of himself as one of the natural elite. It was much more subtle than the mere possession of wealth: it was a deeper social feeling, a sense of being socially established, of possessing attributes—family, education, and refinement—that others lacked, above all, of being accepted by and being able to move easily among those who considered themselves to be the respectable and cultivated. It is perhaps anachronistic to describe this social sense as a class interest, for it often transcended immediate political or economic concerns, and, as Hamilton's argument indicates, was designed to cut through narrow occupational categories. The Republicans of Philadelphia, for example, repeatedly denied that they represented an aristocracy with a united class interest. "We are of different occupations; of different sects of religion; and have different views of life. No factions or private system can comprehend us all." Yet with all their assertions of diversified interests the Republicans were not without a social consciousness in their quarrel with the supporters of the Pennsylvania Constitution. If there were any of us ambitious for power, their apology continued, then there would be no need to change the Constitution, for we surely could attain power under the present Constitution. "We have already seen how easy the task is for *any character* to rise into power and consequence under it. And there are some of us, who think not so meanly of ourselves, as to dread any rivalship from those who are now in office."

In 1787 this kind of elitist social consciousness was brought into play as perhaps never before in eighteenth-century America, as gentlemen up and down the continent submerged their sectional and economic differences in the face of what seemed to be a threat to the very foundations of society. Despite his earlier opposition to the Order of the Cincinnati, Theodore Sedgwick, like other frightened New Englanders, now welcomed the organization as a source of strength in the battle for the Constitution. The fear of social disruption that had run through much of the writing of the eighties was brought to a head to eclipse all other fears. Although state politics in the eighties remains to be analyzed, the evidence from Federalist correspondence indicates clearly a belief that never had there occurred "so great a change in the opinion of the best people" as was occurring in the last few years of the decade. The Federalists were astonished at the outpouring in 1787 of influential and respectable people who had earlier remained quiescent. Too many of "the better sort of people," it was repeatedly said, had withdrawn at the end of the war "from the theatre of public action, to scenes of retirement and ease," and thus "demagogues of desperate fortunes, mere adventurers in fraud, were left to act unopposed." After all, it was explained, "when the wicked rise, men hide themselves." Even the problems of Massachusetts in 1786, noted General Benjamin Lincoln, the repressor of the Shaysites, were not caused by the rebels, but by the laxity of "the good people of the state."

But the lesson of this laxity was rapidly being learned. Everywhere, it seemed, men of virtue, good sense, and property, "almost the whole body of our enlighten'd and leading characters in every state," were awakened in support of stronger government. "The scum which was thrown upon the surface by the fermentation of the war is daily sinking," Benjamin Rush told Richard Price in 1786, "while a pure spirit is occupying its place." "Men are brought into action who had consigned themselves to an eve of rest," Edward Carrington wrote to Jefferson in June 1787, "and the Convention, as a Beacon, is rousing the attention of the Empire." The Antifederalists could only stand amazed at this "weight of talents" being gathered in support of the Constitution. "What must the individual be who could thus oppose them united?"

Still, in the face of this preponderance of wealth and respectability in support of the Constitution, what remains extraordinary about 1787–88 is not the weakness and disunity but the political strength of Antifederalism. That large numbers of Americans could actually reject a plan of government created by a body "compossd of the first characters in the Continent" and backed by Washington and nearly the whole of the natural aristocracy of the country said more about the changing character of American politics and society in the eighties than did the Constitution's eventual acceptance. It was indeed a portent of what was to come.

Delegates to the

Philadelphia Convention

All of the states except Rhode Island appointed delegates to the Convention; Rhode Island ignored the proceedings. The remaining twelve states appointed a total of sixty-five delegates; of these, fifty-five attended the Convention. Sixteen of the fifty-five in attendance either left the Convention before it ended or refused to sign the Constitution. Thus, at the end of the Convention thirty-nine men signed the Constitution. In the list given below, those thirty-nine are indicated by an asterisk.

NEW HAMPSHIRE
John Langdon* • Nicholas Gilman*

MASSACHUSETTS
Elbridge Gerry • Nathaniel Gorham* • Rufus King* • Caleb Strong

CONNECTICUT
William Samuel Johnson* • Roger Sherman* • Oliver Elsworth

NEW YORK
Robert Yates • Alexander Hamilton* • John Lansing

NEW JERSEY
William Livingstone* • David Brearly* • William C. Houston • William Paterson* • Jonathan Dayton*

PENNSYLVANIA
Benjamin Franklin* • Thomas Mifflin* • Robert Morris* • George Clymer* • Thomas Fitzsimons* • Jared Ingersoll* • James Wilson* • Gouverneur Morris*

DELAWARE
George Read* • Gunning Bedford, Jr.* • John Dickinson* • Richard Basset* • Jacob Broom*

MARYLAND
James McHenry* • Daniel of St. Thomas Jenifer* • Daniel Carroll* • John Francis Mercer • Luther Martin

VIRGINIA
George Washington* • Edmund Randolph • John Blair* • James Madison* • George Mason • George Wythe • James McClurg

NORTH CAROLINA
Alexander Martin • William R. Davie • William Blount* • Richard D. Spaight* • Hugh Williamson*

SOUTH CAROLINA
John Rutledge* • Charles C. Pinckney* • Charles Pinckney* • Pierce Butler*

GEORGIA
William Few* • Abraham Baldwin* • William Pierce • William Houstoun

Guide to Further Reading

For a more complete listing of available literature on the period of the Constitution's formation than can be given here, the student should consult Oscar Handlin *et. al.,* eds., *The Harvard Guide to American History* (Cambridge, Mass. 1955) and Roy P. Basler, *et. al.,* eds., *A Guide to the Study of the United States of America* (Washington, 1960). David Hawke's *The Colonial Experience* (Indianapolis, 1966) is a textbook with an especially up-to-date and complete annotated bibliography. Other more specialized bibliographical aids are: Jack P. Greene's introduction to his collection of essays *The Reinterpretation of the American Revolution, 1763–1789* (New York, 1968); another introductory essay which also provides commentary as well as titles will be found in Esmond Wright, ed., *Causes and Consequences of the American Revolution* (Chicago, 1966). Richard B. Morris, *The American Revolution Reconsidered* (New York, 1967) considers the historiography of the 1780s.

Edmund Morgan's *The Birth of the Republic, 1763–89* (Chicago, 1956) is a brief narrative of the entire revolutionary era with its major emphasis on politics. Merrill Jensen's *The Articles of Confederation* (Madison, Wis., 1940) and *The New Nation: A History of the United States, 1781–1789* (New York, 1950) provide a detailed narrative of the Confederation Period which supports Charles Beard's thesis. Forrest McDonald's *E Pluribus Unum: The Formation of the American Republic, 1776–1790* (Boston, 1965) treats the Revolutionary Era as a struggle between state-centered localists and Congressionally-based nationalists (reprinted in paperback as *Formation of the American Republic, 1776–1790*).

Students intrigued by the question, argued implicitly or explicitly by several of the writers presented here, of whether American society was already democratic in the 1780s should look further by consulting Robert E. Brown, *Middle-Class Democracy and the Revolution in Massachusetts, 1691–1780* (Ithaca, N.Y., 1955); Robert E. and B. Katherine Brown, *Virginia, 1705–1786: Democracy or Aristocracy?* (East Lansing, Mich., 1964); Jackson Turner Main, *The Social Structure of Revolutionary America* (Princeton, 1965).

Shays's Rebellion in western Massachusetts in 1786–87 is thought by some to have frightened several of the states into sending delegates to the Philadelphia Convention. It is studied in detail in Robert J. Taylor, *Western Massachusetts in the Revolution* (Providence, R.I. 1954); Marion L. Starkey, *A Little Rebellion* (New York, 1955); and Richard B. Morris, "Insurrection in Massachusetts," in Daniel Aaron, ed., *America in Crisis* (New York, 1952). John C. Ranney in "The Bases of American Federalism," *The William and Mary Quarterly,* 3 s., III, No. 1 (January, 1946), 1–35, examines the various forces and motives leading toward the closer union of the thirteen states in 1787.

The Philadelphia Convention has been described many times. Some of the better treatments are: Max Farrand, *The Framing of the Constitution* (New Haven, 1913); Robert L. Schuyler, *The Constitution of the United States* (New York, 1923); Charles Van Doren, *The Great Rehearsal* (New York, 1948); Charles Warren, *The Making of the Constitution* (Boston, 1928); Clinton Rossiter, *1787, The Grand Convention* (New York, 1966). Catherine Drinker Bowen's *Miracle at Philadelphia* (Boston, 1966) is a popularized account of the meeting.

Biographies of the principal figures at Philadelphia provide a needed dimension for an understanding of the Convention's temper. James Madison has been treated in massive and loving detail by Irving Brant, in his *James Madison: The Nationalist, 1780–1787* (Indianapolis, 1948) and *James Madison: Father of the Constitution, 1787–1800* (Indianapolis, 1950). Similar in size and temper to Brant's study of Madison is Broadus Mitchell's *Alexander Hamilton: Youth to Maturity, 1755–1788* (New York, 1957); shorter and more critical is John C. Miller's *Alexander Hamilton: Portrait in Paradox* (New York, 1959, in pb. as *Alexander Hamilton and the Growth of the New Nation*).

Studying the ratification contests in each of the states is an essential test for any interpretation of the formation of the Constitution. The following studies describe the conflict over the ratification of the Constitution in individual states: Samuel B. Harding, *The Contest over Ratification of the Federal Constitution in the State of Massachusetts* (New York, 1896); Frank G. Bates, *Rhode Island and the Formation of the Union* (New York, 1898). Clarence E. Miner, *Ratification of the Federal Constitution by the State of New York* (New York, 1921) should be checked against the excellent and more recent study by Linda Grant DePauw, *The Eleventh Pillar: New York State and the Federal Constitution* (Ithaca, N.Y., 1966). Pennsylvania's brief contest has been described in detail in J. B. McMaster and F. D. Stone, *Pennsylvania and the Federal Constitution, 1787–1788* (Philadelphia, 1888); a more inclusive modern study by Robert L. Brunhouse sets the ratification controversy within the framework of Pennsylvania's long drawn out contest over her own frame of government, *The Counter-Revolution in Pennsylvania, 1776–1790* (Harrisburg, 1942). Richard P. McCormick's *Experiment in Independence, 1781–1788* (New Brunswick, N.J. 1953) describes the "Critical Period" in New Jersey. Philip Crowl, "Antifederalism in Maryland," *The William and Mary Quarterly*, 3 s., IV (1947), 446–469, treats the controversy in Maryland adequately. Virginia's sharply fought contest was first

described by Hugh B. Grigsby, *The History of the Virginia Federal Convention of 1788* (2 vols., Richmond, Va. 1890–1891). Albert J. Beveridge in his *The Life of John Marshall*, Vol. 1 (Boston, 1916) also treats the Convention. In North Carolina the Beard thesis was applied with inconclusive results by William C. Pool, "An Economic Interpretation of the Ratification of the Federal Constitution in North Carolina," *North Carolina Historical Review*, XXVII (1950), 119–141, 289–313, 437–461.

Much of the source material for a study of the formation of the Constitution has been published. The records of the Philadelphia Convention are found in Max Farrand, ed., *Records of the Federal Convention* (4 vols., New Haven, 1911–37). Charles Callan Tansill, ed., *Documents Illustrative of the Formation of the Union of the American States* (Washington, 1927) is a convenient and comprehensive collection of documents pertaining to all phases of the struggle for the Constitution. Jonathan Elliot, ed., *The Debates in the Several State Conventions on the Adoption of the Federal Constitution* (5 vols., Philadelphia, 1861) is most complete on the ratification struggle in the states. Alexander Hamilton, James Madison and John Jay's contribution to the ratification controversy in New York, *The Federalist*, has been reprinted many times. Jacob Cooke's (Middletown, Conn., 1961) is an excellent complete edition. Cecelia M. Kenyon has done what the Antifederalists should have done during the ratification controversy and collected their most important writings in *The Antifederalists* (Indianapolis, 1966). The introduction to this collection is an enlargement of Miss Kenyon's "Men of Little Faith: The Antifederalists on the Nature of Representative Government," *The William and Mary Quarterly*, 3 s., XII, No. 1 (January, 1955), 3–43. Morton Borden has also edited a collection of Antifederalist writings, *The Antifederalist Papers* (East Lansing, Mich., 1965). A documentary collection which treats only one aspect of the ratification debate is Alpheus Thomas Mason's *The States Rights Debate: Antifederalism and the Constitution* (Englewood Cliffs, N.J., 1964). Robert Allen Rutland's *The Ordeal of the*

Constitution: The Antifederalists and the Ratification Struggle of 1787–1788 (Norman, Oklahoma, 1966) is an excellent complement to Jackson Turner Main's *The Antifederalists* in understanding these contentious critics of the Constitution.

The student who wishes to follow the conflict over Charles Beard's economic interpretation in American historiography will be interested in the following: Howard K. Beale, ed., *Charles A. Beard: An Appraisal* (Lexington, Ky., 1954); Maurice Blinkoff, "The Influence of Charles A. Beard upon American Historiography," University of Buffalo *Studies,* Monographs in History, XII (May, 1936), No. 4; Cecelia M. Kenyon, "*An Economic Interpretation of the Constitution* After Fifty Years," *Centennial Review,* VII (1963), 327–352; Forrest McDonald, *We the People: The Economic Origins of the Constitution* (Chicago, 1958); Robert L. Schuyler, "Forrest McDonald's Critique of the Beard Thesis," *The Journal of Southern History,* XXVIII (1961), 73–80; Jackson Turner Main, "Charles A. Beard and the Constitution: A Critical Review of Forrest McDonald's *We the People,*" *The William and Mary Quarterly,* 3 s., XVII, No. 2 (April, 1961), 86–110; Robert E. Thomas, "A Reappraisal of Charles A. Beard's *An Economic Interpretation of the Constitution of the United States,*" *American Historical Review,* LVII (1951–52), 370–375; Robert E. Brown, *The Reinterpretation of the Formation of the American Constitution* (Boston, 1963); Lee Benson, *Turner and Beard: American Historical Writing Reconsidered* (New York, 1960); Richard Hofstadter, *The Progressive Historians: Turner, Beard, Parrington* (New York, 1969).